Choose Love

How to move through heartache with grace and rise like a phoenix

Heidi Piper

ISBN 978-1-7330351-0-1 (Paperback)

Editing by Mary Lou Kayser and Renee Simas
Front Cover Image by Christos Karapanos
Book Design by Jake Welsh

Printed and bound in the United States of America
First printing October 2019

Published by PhoenixRising, LLC

Visit our website phoenixrisingco.com

To my dear beloved, family and friends, the angels on earth that enabled me to move through heartache with grace and rise like a phoenix. I would not be where I am now without you, and I am so grateful for all you have given me.

Contents

Prologue

MANY OF US ARE being called into significant transitions now, either pushed into them through life circumstances or beckoned into them through a restless feeling that we can and should be doing more with our lives. These transitions can be very challenging. It is not always clear how to move through them at all, let alone do so with grace and end up in a better place than before.

Further, the social structures that used to help us through heartache and difficult transitions do not exist anymore in the way they once did. Our extended family, tribe, village, and community have evolved over generations as we have become more affluent. These traditional, built-in to our lives sources of strength and wisdom are now optional versus required for survival in the time of our ancestors. Consequently, we often end up facing these transitions more alone and with less help than ever before.

If you are at a point in your life where significant transition is calling you, particularly if the call is accompanied by heartache, this book is for you. It shares a set of practices that I believe, based on my own personal experience, can support you to move more easily through heartache and deep transformation. I experienced the power of them personally in deep crisis when my husband left me out of the blue after two decades of marriage. His leaving thrust me into profound grief and my biggest life transition to date. Initially without an extensive support system and with my nervous system convinced it was fighting for my very survival, I instinctively put these practices into place one by one. They have ultimately enabled me to survive and thrive.

My personal mission was born out of this experience. That mission is to help people heal and transform, transcend to the highest version of themselves, and get on the road to doing what they are on the planet to do. I deeply believe choosing love in ways small and big, on a daily basis and in front of the most mammoth life challenges, is a profound key to our healing and happiness. I would love to start a Choose Love movement with you. Concrete ways to participate are offered at the back of this book.

While this is my story, we all have a story. There is a question at the end of every chapter inviting you to consider your story. If you would like to go deeper and start taking concrete steps forward on your own healing and transformation journey, at the end of the book there is an exercise for each chapter with space for you to capture insights and action steps leading to your new future.

I hope my story will support those of you who feel heartache and those who are in front of deep transition to make it through with grace and rise like a phoenix. You are a phoenix. This is a journey map for you to learn to survive, transform, thrive and then fly into the next glorious chapter of life that you are meant to live.

"A wound is the place where the light enters you."
- Rumi

Background:
The making of me
until the breaking of me

THE PAIN OF THE loss of my marriage was excruciating. I was told by a spiritual woman helping me through it that I could have easily subconsciously chosen to die. In fact, she said to me early on in our work together that I needed to be aware it was possible to die of heartache, that my heart could literally stop beating. It was a wake-up call early in my grieving process. I knew I did not want that, that I wanted to live, even though at the time what I was feeling was excruciating. I had never known pain like that.

Up until that fateful day when my husband left our marriage, my life was pretty ordinary, particularly the first few decades. I grew up middle class in the American Midwest. My parents divorced when I was eight, and I spent the next ten years going back and forth between their houses every week with my younger brother. I was not particularly popular in high school; I was one of the 'nerdy artists,' smart and active in theater and speech club. I graduated high school and went on to the University of Illinois to study chemical engineering, following in the footsteps of my dad academically, also an engineer. I liked math and chemistry and loved a challenge, so for me it was a logical choice.

While I was successful academically, as my studies progressed, I began to question whether or not I had chosen the right major. In my third year, I was seriously thinking of changing to communication or advertising. My dad talked me out of it, suggesting I finish, get my engineering degree, then do what I wanted. I decided to follow his advice, which I think was sound, even with 30 years of hindsight.

That summer I was hired for a research and development internship at a major consumer products company. Upon graduation, they offered me full-time employment. While they recruited chemical engineers for my role, the job interfaced heavily with marketing and required consumer understanding to design products and innovation pipelines. The people there were great and the work was interesting, so I decided to try it. I moved to Ohio to work. My college sweetheart moved there to join me, and we were married shortly thereafter.

A year and a half later I felt restless at work and asked for a transfer to Europe. As a backup to going to Europe, I applied to get my MBA at The Kellogg School of Business in Evanston, Illinois. The company hesitated to send me overseas. They had never sent an employee as young as I was on an international assignment. I was 24 at the time. After six months of back and forth discussion, six weeks before the start of the MBA program, and me being clear that I would leave to get my MBA if it was not possible to go overseas, they agreed.

I really could not tell you where my motivation to go to Europe came from. It was like a very subtle whisper, an inner subconscious knowing, that that was what I needed to do next. I can't say I thought much about where it was coming from or why I wanted to do it, but it felt like it was the right, next thing for me. In hindsight it was odd, as I had never been overseas, had never held a passport, and had never before been interested in traveling abroad. The feeling emerged that I needed to travel and learn languages and broaden my perspective. It was a life goal, not a work goal. In my mind, working there was a means to that end.

My director at work asked me where I wanted to go - Newcastle, England or Brussels, Belgium. I looked at a map and immediately chose Brussels. It was more centrally located in Europe than Newcastle, and they did not have English as one of their official languages; therefore, I could more easily achieve my objectives of traveling and learning languages. My husband was happy to go on the adventure as well, so we packed up our few things and moved to Belgium without ever having been there.

I was in heaven. The first three years I was pinching my cheek, asking myself if it was real. It felt like a fairy tale. I loved the diversity and the fantastic food - Belgium has a huge international community and Belgians are real foodies. Everything they make is amazing! I loved the beautiful, quaint countryside, hidden monasteries making beer and wine, the Art Deco architecture, and frequently visiting Paris and London a few hours away by train. I think we went to Paris 12 times in the first year and traveled all over Europe in those first three years by car using our ample, annual 30 days of European vacation time.

Three years passed. My husband wanted to return to the US and move back to Chicago to live near his family and ultimately raise a family there. However, I could not see myself leaving Europe. Again, I had an inner knowing, a feeling that I had to stay there, at least for a while. We ended up separating and getting divorced amicably. We had no children, just a few material possessions to divide, and were able to do it without hiring lawyers.

The man who would become my next husband is beautiful, sweet, smart and a tall, dark, handsome Italian. He took my breath away. I met him at work. He was working for my office mate, so he was often in and out of our two-person office. We got to know each other over lunch. Usually, the whole team went to lunch together; oddly, however, for a couple of months no one else wanted to go for lunch, so it was just the two of us. We became friends and then became a couple. He was a careful person in general, as was I. I did not want to get divorced again, so it took us two and a half years to start living together and another two years to get married. We had a beautiful, small wedding in his hometown in Italy.

A year later I got pregnant. When I was six months along, we went to the US to visit my parents. A mutual friend had reconnected me with my childhood best friend, Sarah, a neurologist working at the hospital in our hometown. While shopping, I felt intense pains in my belly and went home to call her to ask for her gynecologist's number so I could get checked. She asked me a few questions, one of which was, "How often are the pains occurring?" I answered, "Every five minutes." She told me I should go to the hospital to get checked, and she would meet me there.

Since I was only six months pregnant with my first baby, I had not done the birthing classes yet and had no idea what was going on. I am also an optimist, so it did not occur to me that I was in labor (yes, I know it should have been self-evident, but I was in it and could not see the forest for the trees). Sarah knew but did not tell me to ensure I stayed calm. When I arrived at the hospital, she had already checked me in.

They wheeled me into a delivery room, which I did not know was a delivery room as it looked like any other room. As I was changing into my gown, I noticed I was bleeding. I later learned this is typical at that stage of labor. At that point, I was glad I was there. Long story short, our son was born four hours later after they tried to stop the labor and the doctor told me I would not leave the hospital until the baby was born. I recall hearing myself say in my head, *I am not spending 12 more weeks hanging out in a hospital 5000 miles from home!* Not that I wanted to have him right then, but I preferred to hang out at home while I waited. Nonetheless, he was destined to enter the world that night.

Our son was 25% bigger than he should have been at that gestational age at two pounds, 12 ounces, which was lucky. His entire hand could not fit around one of our fingers. He was breathing on his own, occasionally, which was typical for babies that age. He was in the intensive care unit for 50 days, where he steadily grew and learned how to breathe on his own. He survived and thrived. He was a tough fighter who chose life, particularly at three weeks old when he got a yeast infection in his blood. It took the medical staff two spinal taps, multiple blood draws, and a lot of lab work over two days to identify the strain of infection. His doctor was then able to administer targeted treatment, but by then our baby boy had started healing himself. He is now a young adult and an amazing old soul, 6'4", smart, handsome and extremely healthy. His entry into the world was scary, and I am so grateful he is my son and that he chose life.

Three years later our wonderful daughter came along. She too was impatient to enter this world, although she made it longer through the pregnancy than her brother did. She was born in Belgium at seven and a half months gestational age. At five pounds, she was nearly double our son's birth weight but still considered premature. The nurses in the intensive care unit saw how comfortable we were taking care of her. Consequently, they let her come home after ten days, sending a nurse practitioner to visit once a week for the next six weeks to ensure we had the support we needed. She is now a young adult, smart and beautiful, intensely determined, and very capable. I am so grateful that she is my daughter.

The following years in Belgium were a happy blur. I call them the golden years. The kids were happy, healthy and growing. We bought and extensively renovated a house that I loved. We both kept working for our company and made remarkable career progress, quickly moving into executive leadership positions.

After 19 years in Belgium, the company asked us to move to enable continued career development. We agreed to relocate to Germany, taking on additional responsibilities.

We decided to take two months off between Belgium and Germany to travel the Pacific Northwest of the United States and Canada with the kids. We went by car, boat, and RV and drank up the immense beauty. I love nature, and we hit the jackpot there. It was a wonderful time for the family.

When we arrived in Germany, our daughter entered first grade and our son, fourth. They attended an excellent international school and settled in well. The next eight years were filled with the kids going to school, my husband and me going to work, lots of work-related travel all over the world for me, some international work travel for my husband, and many trips away every year for the whole family. We went to the US and Italy to see family and to warm places we could scuba dive and enjoy the intense sun that I missed living in Germany. Life was good.

I loved my work, and particularly the community we had created at work, as well as the tough challenges we solved together regularly. Over time, however, I was starting to feel like something was missing from my life, and that continuing to do what I was doing day in and day out was not enough.

I also started feeling my husband searching for more. Mentally, he was less present at home. While we spent a lot of time together and still had long conversations about work, life and the kids, the level of romantic connection we had was not the same as before. We'd had periods of stronger and weaker romantic connection through the years, which I assumed were the result of the inherent ebb and flow of a long-term marriage. This felt different though. I was feeling more and more isolated and lonely.

We had been expats for twenty-five years. I had a big job, as did he. I was committed to being the best mother I could be to our kids. I was lucky in that we had a sufficiently flexible schedule at work that I could manage my day in the way I needed to be present at the kids' functions at school, and we had an after-school nanny until we got home from work. We are both introverts and loved being just the four of us at home, so we did not end up creating a robust social life. I had a few close friends, but they lived far away. While we were raised Catholic, we were not religious and had no other spiritual practice, although we raised the kids with strong morals. In short, we were isolated from our family and friends, with a tightly bonded nuclear family and no spiritual community or practice.

I read a Power Path newsletter from Jose and Lena Stevens every month, something I have done for 25 years. It outlines the month ahead, key trends to expect and personal, internal work that is suggested considering these trends. I remember reading at this time that we are at a critical point in our history as a human community and that we urgently need to significantly step up our level of consciousness to enable the survival of our species and our planet. This resonated with me.

In December of 2015, I recall lying on my bed resting mid-afternoon, feeling sad, feeling like somehow there was not enough love in general in my life and wanting to help with whatever we needed as humans to evolve. I felt like I was supposed to help but had no idea how. I sent up a request to what I feel is the greater power that supports us, which I call 'The Universe,' that it be made clear to me what I am supposed to do to help, offering that I was ready to help.

Four weeks later, out of the blue, my husband told me he was leaving me after nearly 20 years of marriage and 24 years together. It was a devastating shock. He had never said he was unhappy. He said he did not want to work on the marriage; he simply wanted out of it.

That was three years ago. I went through a very difficult journey and have now come out the other side into a completely different, happy life. I grew by leaps and bounds. So much has changed and for the better. I have so much more love in my life, more and stronger relationships with family and friends and my partner. I wrote, recorded, and published an original music album and have now written and published this, my first book. I have completely changed my career to one where I aim to serve others and support their growth and started my own company to enable doing so. I moved to a beautiful place I love, a place that feels like *my* place, in a community where I really feel at home. And I am deeply grateful every day.

I learned so much along this journey about how to heal from the pain of a traumatic life event, how to create a life full of joy and how to achieve my dreams. I now know that no matter how hard it seems, this is possible. This book attempts to share with you what I learned in the hope that it can support your journey to heal, find yourself again, and get back on the road to blissfully doing what you are on the planet to do. For the rest of the story, read on.

You are only a victim if you choose to be. Do not choose victimhood; choose love, for others and for yourself. You create your reality. You are the architect of your life. You are at a crossroads now. What life will you design and build?

CHAPTER 1

Choose Love

"Darkness cannot drive out darkness; only light can do that.
Hate cannot drive out hate; only love can do that."
- Martin Luther King Jr.

"One word frees us of all the weight and pain of life: that
word is love." - Sophocles

I COULD NOT BELIEVE my husband was leaving. While I had
felt him a little distant and had realized through some of our interactions over the holidays that our marriage was having trouble, I did not expect him to leave. His parents had been married
for nearly 50 years and role modeled well the love and effort
required to make a long, strong marriage. They had solid family
values which he seemed to embody, and he is a good person.
We had a strong friendship and partnership underlying the marriage. But despite all this, he was leaving. I was devastated.

He told me while we were out in the woods, a place we spent a lot of time walking and biking together. It was January. I recall returning home and starting to shake uncontrollably, freezing not from the cold but from the shock. I did not know how to stop it. I instinctively filled the bathtub with hot water and got in it. I think I had taken two tub baths in the ten years we were in that house, and this was one of them.

I spent the following weeks on the couch crying, wrapped in a blanket that his parents had given me for my birthday two months earlier, which they brought from Cusco, Peru. The kids, then 17 and 13, were also upset and coping as best they could.

I went to work during the day and did not tell anyone what had happened. My husband and I worked in the same office and were two of the most senior leaders there. I was worried people would gossip; I did not want or need the additional emotional stress that that would bring. Despite my best efforts to hide what was happening, however, my coworkers could tell something was wrong. I was not my usual passionate, happy self.

Thankfully, they respected my privacy. When they asked if I was okay and I said I was okay in a way that was clear I was really not but preferred not to talk about it, they compassionately let it be. I ran a global organization of over 100 people, and they relied on me for decisions and support every day. I loved the people I worked with and, frankly, being at work was a welcome distraction. Sadness was underlying everything I did, however, and it was heavily present every night when I went home.

I recall reading something during that time about how anger at someone else is like eating rat poison and expecting it to kill the other person. I already felt more physically and emotionally devastated than I had ever felt in my life. I did not want to do anything else to make it worse for the kids or me, so I decided I would 'choose love' towards my husband in this situation. I decided to not say anything negative about him to him or anyone else. Not to blame him, not to express anger, not to be bitter. I still loved him and knew that we had an underlying bond and that we cared about each other no matter what happened in the end. And I did not want to take the rat poison. I could not handle any more pain as I was barely hanging on.

He met me there in that space of love. I think he expected much worse. A few months after he left, we were taking a walk and talking. Reacting to my calm demeanor, he asked, "Who are you?" He continued to say I was behaving in a way most people would not. I told him I did not want to do anything to create more pain. Two years later, he was still coming over for dinner every week and helping at the house as needed, despite the fact that he was already living with his girlfriend. He told me people were asking him why he was doing these things. They did not understand. I believe this happened as the result of my choosing love and his responding in kind.

Choosing love supported me, my kids, and my husband in many wonderful ways. We continued to spend time together each week as a family and spent holidays together the year after he left. We only got a lawyer for our divorce because we had to do so by law in Germany and then we just got one lawyer between us. When we learned that one of us would have to file for the divorce legally, I told him he should be the one since he was the one who wanted to end the marriage. He agreed. The lawyer then said to us that they could only represent one client legally, not both, and the one filing for divorce had to have a lawyer. He agreed again and said, "Okay, but you need to make sure she is taken care of, too."

They looked at us and said, "Who are you? We never see this."

We told them what we wanted in terms of separating our things, which we wrote down on a piece of paper one afternoon, sitting on the patio of our house.

Eighteen months after he left, we took our son together from Germany to the US to college. I went with our daughter to visit his parents nearly two and a half years after he left. We still co-parent seamlessly.

Choosing love might sound impossible when you are suffering so intensely as a result of the choices of another. My experience, however, was that it was the biggest key to surviving and then thriving. This one uncommon choice, choosing to react with love in the face of being heartbroken by the person I loved, was likely the most important choice I made that enabled the rest of this story. It is possible for us to choose to stay in the space where love lives, mentally and with our words and actions. The space of kind thoughts, words and actions for others and for ourselves. In the face of opposition, what thoughts, words or actions can you choose today that live where love lives?

CHAPTER 2

Get Emotional Support

"Call it a clan, call it a network, call it a family, whatever you call it, whoever you are, you need one." - Jane Howard

"If you don't have the relationships you need in your life, go out and build them. You are the one you are waiting for." - Heidi Piper

TRAUMA CAN BE DOUBLY difficult when it triggers childhood wounds. Not only do we suffer what happened, but we also re-suffer childhood trauma on top of it. Time helped me understand that I had suffered a double whammy when my husband left. As a child, I often felt unseen and unloved, particularly by my mother, who was dealing with her own childhood wounds in the best way she could. Part of her coping strategy was attaching herself firmly, and what felt like preferentially, to my younger brother. I remember feeling intense and painful loneliness. Losing my marriage triggered this old deep wound, making the pain even more extreme than it already was. Perhaps in an instinctive will to survive, I reached out to a small circle of people close to me for emotional support.

I had been talking to my dad and my stepmom on the phone for an hour or so once every few weeks for years. As my marriage dissolved, we agreed to talk every week at a set time. Of course, I could call them if I needed to in-between. While Sarah and I had been spending a week together every six months on vacation for years with our families, we did not often talk on the phone. After my husband left, she called me every week to check in. Although the kids were older, we still had a nanny, Maria, who drove them to their activities when needed and helped around the house. She was an angel, even more so during this time. She was emotionally supportive and very empathetic; she left loving, encouraging sticky notes for me on my bedside table to discover when I got home after she'd gone.

My friend Emily from work provided emotional support every time we connected 1-1. She invited me to come stay with her and her family when I would travel to Geneva for business. I reached out to a woman, Lisa, whom I had also become friends with through work. She eventually became one of my closest friends and provided a tremendous amount of support and encouragement.

I started running once a week with my neighbor, Konny, who also offered a lot of emotional support and advice during our runs and occasional outings. I recall one ridiculous conversation we had where we were trying to decide if it was worse having your husband, whom you knew loved you, die (as happened to her), or having your husband leave you because he no longer loved you like he used to (as happened to me).

Konny introduced me to her friend, Monika, who also became a very dear friend and extraordinary support for me daily. Monika's husband had left her in precisely the same manner as mine had, after 20 years of marriage and two kids, and in precisely the same month. While I was worried about the possibility we would drag each other down in our grief when I first met her, we became very close; we were able to grieve and support each other as we knew what it was like to be in each other's shoes. We were also able to inspire each other to be in the situation with courage and love.

Shortly after meeting each other, right before Christmas and nearly a year after my husband left, Monika left me a small Christmas gift at my home. This gift turned out to provide powerful support, well beyond what I suspect she consciously expected, as follows:

A few days after Christmas my husband and I decided to take off our wedding rings, which we had both continued to wear the first year apart. This was very painful for me. I decided to do it before flying to visit my parents. I took off my wedding and engagement rings, then decided to open Monika's gift. She had given me a beautiful necklace. When I put it on, I cried. It made me feel like I was not alone. It symbolized for me that she and others cared for me. I wore it every day for the next year, and it is still a precious gift that I will always be grateful for and cherish.

At work, I also told one human resources person that things were not going well at home. She was amazing. She could sense how much I was suffering and asked me to have coffee every week with her where she listened and offered emotional support.

Eleven months passed before I told her any more of the story and in those 11 months, she sat with me, asking me how I was and metaphorically holding my hand. I was so grateful. I remember telling her later how being at work, in such pain with no one knowing, was weird as I was suffering in silence amongst people who care. Unlike someone who had been in an accident and had significant physical damage, I did not have wounds that others could see. After a person gets in an accident, emotional support flows automatically. In my case, I would have had to tell people about it and ask for support, which wasn't in my nature to do.

In hindsight, I should have shared sooner with more people what was happening. When I did finally tell people close to me at work, the amount of support was overwhelming. Some people even cried. More than two years later I learned I had colleagues who had not yet heard what happened at all, a sign that no one was gossiping, but instead offering genuine empathy and caring.

In the end, despite not telling many people for nearly a year, I was able to build an emotional support network that provided enough of a container for me to do the rest of my personal healing work. Through regular, sometimes even scheduled, connections with my family and friends far away, and through reaching out for new friendships where I shared my story and grief openly, I had a different person lined up each day of the week whom I could connect with. These beautiful souls listened and offered words of perspective and love to help me move through the pain and then start healing.

And, while I genuinely believe that it is not our kids' role to help us with things like this, my kids supported me nonetheless by being present and loving and sometimes with words of great wisdom. One night my son walked into my room and asked how I was doing. I told him, "I'm okay, but I'm having trouble sleeping."

He said, "I recently saw a movie where there was a king and his baby son. The baby son was very sick, but he was sleeping in his father's arms. The king said, 'He is ill, but he is sleeping soundly because he knows he is loved.' Mom, you can sleep, because you are so loved, by me and by so many others."

I believe that we are not meant to go through emotional trauma and deep transition alone. We need to reach out and ask for help. This help can come from family, friends, colleagues or even strangers that then later become great friends. Who can you reach out to that you are already close to or that could perhaps with time become a friend?

CHAPTER 3

Get Professional Support

"As therapists, we are in the business of freedom - we help people relinquish stories of self that are painful, stories of this moment that are alienating, stories of the future that are limiting." - Ili Rivera Walter

"Most of us were not taught how to recognize pain, name it and be with it." - Brene Brown

AT WORK, I TOLD my boss straightaway that I was having trouble at home and needed to stop traveling for a while. I had been traveling a lot for work and had an unprecedented amount of travel booked the majority of the month ahead. She was great. She said she only needed me to travel one day that month and the rest I could handle from the office. She told her boss, who was fantastic too. He also said I did not need to travel, that the whole organization was so well connected virtually that joining conversations remotely would be fine. And he asked me what I needed, including if I needed to move or have a different job. I was overwhelmed with the support from both of them.

My boss also asked if I wanted to get help from a professional therapist. She noted that the company supports the first few sessions and that they outsource the service to preserve confidentiality for the employee. I was not convinced that it would help; however, she encouraged me, and I decided to try. Because we were in Germany and my German was intermediate at best, I called the service and asked for an English-speaking therapist. When you are in pain, you do not want to have to search for words - it's hard enough to articulate in your own language what you feel.

They connected me to an Irish psychologist. I have to confess that, at first, I was mostly interested in seeing a therapist as those in my support system at the time all lived in other countries, and I wanted to sit in front of a human to talk about what was happening and feel the emotional support. She was energetic and somewhat intense, and I was unsure at first if it was going to work. I have to say though that I saw her for nearly two and a half years, and it became more and more powerful over the course of that time. I relaxed and as she got to know me better, she shared more of her perspective more openly; she often said what I needed to hear and helped me make the most effective choices about what to do next. I still hear her advice in my head sometimes when I get triggered. In that way, she continues helping me make good choices today.

At the same time, I reached out for help from a woman I had met at work 10 years earlier. The company had hired her to help create high-performing teams within the context of our innovation workshop. I knew she also worked with individuals and couples in her practice, however, and I instinctively felt she could help me. While 73 years old, and self-described as a '107-year-old Tibetan elf,' Mu was usually extremely busy traveling and working all over the world and would not have had time to take me on as a client. But as fate or divine intervention would have it, she had had surgery and was at home recovering, so she had time to work with me.

Our relationship became an incredibly powerful one for me for many reasons. Mu laid the groundwork for significant growth and life shifts I would make in the coming years, midwifing, if you will, my rebirth. A somatic healer, she taught me to feel into my body again, to be constantly aware of what it was telling me. She showed me my original pain from this life and helped me to release it. She taught me how to love my inner child and help heal myself. She supported my emerging meditation practice and so much more. We worked together primarily through video connect, although I would see her face to face from time to time.

After a couple of months, she suggested I come to her house in Boulder, Colorado, to work together for three days straight, to speed the healing process. I agreed to go. It was a profound weekend with a powerful range of healing modalities but, above all, it was a safe, loving place to grieve.

My ex-colleague and friend Daniel had been at Mu's with his wife the weekend before. I did not know they had been there and had not talked to Daniel for a long time. When I walked into the room at her house where I was going to sleep, I found a handwritten note from Daniel for me. He said he did not know what was happening to me, but if I was at Mu's to work with her, I must be going through something significant. He wrote that he wanted me to know he was sending me love and supporting my healing from whatever I was dealing with. I sat on the bed and cried. When people expressed love and support during this time, it touched me profoundly. Sometimes I thought my husband leaving had cracked me open. It did, which was very painful, but it also let love from others permeate me more deeply.

That weekend I also discovered Boulder in my free time. It was March and snowy. I looked up online what to do in Boulder, and hiking the Chautauqua trail was the top recommendation. I put on my boots and went to Chautauqua Park to hike. The moment I walked onto the field that leads from the park to the mountain trail and looked up at the Flatiron Mountains in front of me, I felt an intense sensation of bliss and peace - like I was home. This place seemed magical to me. It was a piece of land that felt familiar, comfortable, safe and healing. It is the only place I have ever been that I feel deeply connected to besides the Northern Minnesota lake I have visited every summer since childhood. I still go hiking in the Flatirons when I need to feel connected to something more significant, to soothe myself or to elevate my mood.

Over time Mu became like family to me. She was always watching out for me. The day my husband and I got divorced, she was coincidentally already planning to be in Germany for work and staying at my house. She insisted on coming to the divorce proceeding. She sat in the back, the only person there not directly involved, and witnessed. When we finished and went out to the parking lot, she asked my husband and me to face each other and say one at a time to each other an ancient Hawaiian prayer, Ho'oponopono, "I love you, I am sorry, please forgive me and thank you." Its meaning is to make something right, to restore balance. It promotes both personal responsibility and forgiveness of the other. We did it. It felt like a good ritual. We all went back to the house, where Mu disappeared to leave us some space; my husband and I had coffee and talked. When he got up to leave, he looked at me and spontaneously repeated the prayer, gave me a hug, and left.

There are many professionals available to help us through our most difficult times. They can offer a meaningful sounding board and compassionate, supportive human contact when we really need it. And they can teach us skills that we can use the rest of our lives. It does not have to include a long-term commitment. Sometimes even one good conversation can unlock things in a way that really helps to make progress. Who do you know that might provide a reference for someone to reach out to for help?

CHAPTER 4

Mourn

"We must accept sadness as an appropriate, natural stage of loss. Grief transforms the broken, wounded soul."
- Elisabeth Kübler-Ross and David Kessler

"Grief is not a disorder, a disease or a sign of weakness.
It is an emotional, physical and spiritual necessity, the price you pay for love. The only cure for grief is to grieve."
- Earl Grollman

ONE THING THAT MU and a number of my friends taught me was that I needed to open up to the grief. I could count on one hand the number of times I had cried in the thirty years before my husband left me. I was not prone to tears except during the sad parts of romantic movies and somehow, perhaps, felt crying was unnecessary and likely to lead to feeling pain even more deeply.

They all encouraged me to cry. So over time, hearing my friends say crying was all right, I gave myself permission to cry. Lisa sang me a line from a song she remembered from childhood, "Crying gets the sad out." Someone told me it helps to unblock and move the stuck energy. Mu would hold the space when I started to cry and quietly say, "Yes." And my friend Emily told me that the best way to deal with the pain is to go right through it.

My therapist echoed this sentiment, suggesting that all the time we spend not facing and going through the pain makes the healing process take longer. In fact, I have since learned that any negative or uncomfortable feeling can recede very quickly if you acknowledge and sit with it, fully accepting it for at least 10 seconds. This fits the general concept of what one resists seems to only grow stronger. I think we as humans naturally resist painful feelings, and following the idea mentioned, those feelings then hang around, sometimes indefinitely and become stronger. It's like we need to hear, feel and befriend our pain for it to recede.

So I decided to embrace crying when I feel sad. I cried buckets of tears over the two years after my husband left. I cried for losing my marriage, for the dissolution of our nuclear family as it had been, for the future we would not share together, for the loss of inclusion in my husband's family in the way I had been (although we are still connected and they have shared that I am always welcome). And I cried for my original wound from childhood, for the loneliness, for feeling unloved and unseen, for feeling 'not enough.' Over time, the pain receded, the spells of crying and grief were fewer and farther between, and I became happier little by little.

Giving myself permission to cry was huge. Visualizing crying as simply moving energy that was otherwise blocked facilitated that permission. And thinking my pain would just get worse if I did not deal with it was a very important motivator to get on with grieving. We should not ignore or shut down our grief. We should do our best to acknowledge our pain, face it, embrace it and go right through it. If you could think about your pain as a valuable, temporary part of you, a visitor, what would you do to acknowledge it, be with it and walk alongside it until it subsides?

CHAPTER 5

Take Care of Your Body

"Our bodies are our gardens to which our wills are gardeners." - William Shakespeare

"Take care of your body. It is the only place you will ever live." - Jim Rohn

IN THE MONTHS AFTER my husband left, I instinctively knew that I was dealing with something I was barely capable of handling. While I love the tub of ice-cream with a spoon as a go-to mood enhancer as much as anyone else, when I get depressed, I lose my appetite. At first, I did not want to eat and ate little. But then I understood this was not a short-term phase and felt the best chance to get through it without my body also collapsing was to eat as healthy as possible.

Overnight I dropped alcohol, as it was tempting to use it to numb the pain, as well as sugar, salt, and caffeine. I started drinking a lot of hot tea. It was soothing, and this was also helpful as over the coming months we had the worst weather we had had in my eight years in Germany. It was continually gray, cold, and wet. I ate vegetables and lean protein primarily and drank tea and water for months. I lost 30 pounds and three dress sizes, which boosted my confidence. I was 52 and very unexpectedly, found myself at my ideal weight. And I was healthy. I care deeply about my health and always have, and the shift in my diet, along with the emotional support I was getting from my friends and family, was critical to maintaining my health. In fact, I never got sick in any way after my husband left, which still feels like a miracle.

I was, however, incapable of sleeping through the night. Either I would struggle to fall asleep, or I would fall asleep, only to wake a few hours later and be incapable of falling asleep again. As I was still working full time and taking care of my teenage kids and the house, I knew I needed more sleep than a few hours a night to stay healthy.

My friend Sarah, a sleep doctor, suggested I take sleeping pills. Now I am someone who doesn't like to take any medicine. I will only take a pain reliever if I have intolerable pain, which rarely happens. Funnily enough, I do recall instinctively taking aspirin and putting it in my pocket when I had an incredibly intense fit of emotional pain early on. It's like I needed a pain reliever for the emotional pain and, subconsciously, I reached for aspirin as the only pain reliever I knew. I did realize a little later that was ridiculous and did not take it. I was worried that I would become addicted to the sleeping pills and did not want to take them if that was a risk, but Sarah reassured me the ones she recommended were not addictive. So I started taking them every night and could finally get at least six hours of sleep, enough to get me through the next day. Every few weeks I would try to sleep a night without them. It took me five months to be able to do so, and then I stopped taking them with no issues.

I have been a runner most of my life and a regular runner the past fifteen years or so. I maintained my schedule of running three miles, three to four days a week and a longer, at least a five-mile run, on the weekend. I switched, however, from treadmill running to running in the forest next to the house. This was a powerful change to my routine. On sunny mornings, I got a dose of sunshine, fresh air, and the healing power of being in nature while I exercised. Nature is neutral; it supports and heals you. You can take all your problems there and release them and then take in nature's support.

There is a growing understanding of the power of nature to heal and, in fact, some talk about spending time in nature as 'nature bathing.' As I became more and more aware of nature's capacity to heal, I expressed gratitude more regularly to the woods for supporting me. I found a specific tree which was on the loop I ran that attracted my attention, and I would stop and connect to it every time I passed. It became a comforting ritual through which I felt even more support, knowing that the trees are connected themselves, networked through their root systems across the forest.

I am also a kinesthetic person and need a frequent, consistent dose of human touch. Hugging is not a common practice in Europe among colleagues and friends as it's seen as a very intimate gesture. I always found that odd as they kiss each other on the cheeks, even strangers, and that seems more intimate to me. In any case, my experience was that many Germans do not tend to hug those outside their close circle, so I was not getting hugs outside of my immediate family. My son is kinesthetic, a champion hugger and hugs were free-flowing with him, but he headed off to college, and with my husband not around I was really missing abundant human touch.

Mu suggested I get a massage weekly to help. I found an amazing woman, very reasonably priced, who was located near my home; I went to her for the next two years. She was Thai, my age, and spoke broken English. I finally found a way to explain to her what she had done for me before I left Germany two years later. She had made a significant contribution to my healing, for which I was very grateful. She was very moved and appreciated that I had shared with her my story and the healing gift I felt she had given me.

Finally, I have been curious for a long time about energy healing and started learning about the chakras and how to balance my chakras energetically. I took a short course online that I found through a Facebook ad. By the end of the class, I was able to balance my chakras in a minute, which I would then do every time I felt out of balance or blocked in any way.

Next, I learned about tapping, a great method to relieve intense emotional pain temporarily. Using acupressure points and specific phrases relevant to the issue at hand, you tap points on your face and shoulder area with the tips of your fingers and say particular phrases related to what you are feeling. I learned through seeing a video on YouTube on the subject with tapping expert Nick Ortner and motivational author and publisher Louise Hay. I was reassured it was effective by stories I had heard of soldiers with post-traumatic stress disorder using it to manage their nervous system. I tried it; it helped; and I used it extensively several times a day the first six months to help relieve the emotional pain.

In summary, diet, sleep, exercise, being outdoors in nature, massage and learning simple things I could do myself to manage my 'energy body' and my nervous system were critical to supporting my health and healing as I recovered. Taking the best possible care of ourselves through establishing these nurturing and supportive habits provides the foundation we need to move forward with the rest of our journey. It is an important way to choose love for ourselves. What are one or two things you can do for yourself to strengthen your support for your body?

CHAPTER 6

Meditate

"The thing about meditation is: You become more and more you." - David Lynch

"To a mind that is still, the whole universe surrenders."
- Anonymous

"The goal of meditation isn't to control your thoughts; it's to stop letting them control you." - Anonymous

I HAD WANTED TO meditate for a long time but never managed to muster the discipline to learn and practice consistently. And I thought that my hyperactive mind would not be able to still itself sufficiently to ever be good at meditation. When I found myself in the middle of trauma, I decided it might be a good idea to try again, thinking it might help.

I found an online app, Omvana, where the founder, Vishen Lakhiani, had recorded a meditation called '6 Phase.' I then found an online speech he made at a conference to introduce it and lead the audience through it. This helped me understand why he created it as he did, which helped me lean into it. The meditation was only twenty minutes long and guided, perfect for me. It included a combination of relaxation, gratitude, compassion, forgiveness, visualization for three years out and the coming day, and a blessing. Since I did not need to still my mind, just follow along with what he was saying to do, it was easy. And it really helped.

I practiced that meditation every day for nearly a year and still do it sometimes. It can be done anywhere; I even did it when I was running or (eyes open) driving. I really believe it helped me to become more at peace, more centered, more loving, to start to get clear about what I want for the future, and to create a great day for myself. I think it also helped me to start sleeping naturally.

Wanting to go deeper into meditation, I took a course online from author and personal development and spiritual teacher Deborah King. This was also very helpful to grow as a meditator, and I feel it contributed to me 'waking up' spiritually. She taught a sequence of phrases to use at the end of the meditation to help yourself open up. At this point, I started feeling a powerful tingling sensation in my heart area while I was waking up in the morning or even still sleeping, sometimes so strong that it woke me up. At first, it was a little scary, but with time, I got used to it. While I am still not sure what it means, I think it is also part of my spiritual awakening.

While my meditation practice is still growing and evolving, I have come to understand it a bit better now. When I was a beginner, I saw it like gym training for my brain. I find that analogy helpful as, like with exercise for the body, there are so many different kinds of meditation; there is not a 'one-size-fits-all' kind of med-itation. I needed to try many different ones to find the types that worked best for me personally. I also find it helpful to 'cross train,' using different kinds of meditation at different times. I can flex the training to the time, focus, and circumstances I have available each day. I can meditate sitting, lying down, walking, running or driving. I can meditate for two minutes or an hour, four times a week or three times a day. I can do stillness, grati-tude, compassionate, visioning, body awareness focused and so many other types of meditation. I can do it alone or with others, in person or virtually. Further, like with body training, one gets stronger with practice. The fact that a regular meditation routine is called a meditation practice fits, as I am practicing meditation when I do it!

I even got a meditation buddy to help me maintain my commit-ment to regular practice. I met Astrid at an American Chamber of Commerce conference in Leiden, Germany. We decided to go see an art exhibit together one afternoon. During our visit, we started telling each other our life stories and when we both talk-ed about wanting to have a strong meditation practice, we agreed to be meditation buddies. While we lived an hour apart and only saw each other a handful of times after that, we would text each other every day to check in and share that we had meditated. To continue the gym workout analogy, as with a gym buddy, a medi-tation buddy helped me keep the commitment to daily practice. I knew she was waiting to hear that I had meditated. And know-ing she was doing it too helped motivate me to do it even on the days I did not really feel like it. This daily exchange lasted for more than a year. Astrid became a good friend through this, and we are still in regular contact today.

As I practiced more, the gifts from my meditation grew. It opened access to stronger intuition, greater levels of presence and calm, more love in all my interactions with others and myself, and the certainty inside myself that we are not alone. Meditation is such a powerful, personal tool to strengthen ourselves that I am pretty convinced we will arrive at a time in the not-too-distant future when the majority of us will not think of starting our day without meditation. I would be so bold to suggest that meditation will become a brain/consciousness health hygiene habit much like regularly brushing our teeth or taking a shower are body health hygiene habits.

Workplaces are already starting to recognize the benefits of meditation. In fact, I recently heard that 40% of the top 100 companies now offer meditation or mindfulness training to their employees. I had personally benefited from meditation so much that I wanted to share it at work too. I could see that the middle managers were extremely stressed out. In the hierarchy, they have to 'manage up' their leaders and 'manage down' their staff, really carrying a heavy load. I asked my HR colleagues and a few peers who co-led the 1000-person strong work site with me if they would support me bringing meditation training into the middle management group as an experiment. They readily agreed.

I hired Mu, a decade's-long meditator herself, to come in and teach it. She created a course and taught it over a full year to a group of 22 middle managers. The results were very impressive. While the immediate feedback was in the area of improved health and sleep, in the end, the number one benefit they reported was less negative reactivity at work. They were able to 'watch the movie' and 'be in the movie' at the same time, realizing what they were feeling in the moment and creating enough time between the feeling and how they reacted, to consciously choose what to say and do in a way that nurtured instead of hurt relationships. While my path into meditation was personal, after having this experience, I am also sold on the benefits of meditation at work.

In the end, I am very grateful that I now have a daily meditation practice and for the many gifts it has given me. I wholeheartedly recommend it as a tool to help heal, open up to life and love, and build a tremendous resilience to whatever life brings. There are many ways to meditate and so many free, on-line tools; there is really something for everyone. It may take a little trial and error to find what works best for you, and what works for you may evolve over time. Just dive in and try different options until you find the right practice for you! What option sounds most interesting to try first?

CHAPTER 7

Practice Gratitude

"There are only two ways to live your life. One is as though nothing is a miracle. The other is as though everything is a miracle." - Albert Einstein

"A grateful person is a powerful person, for gratitude generates power. All abundance is based on being grateful for what you have." - Elisabeth Kübler-Ross and David Kessler

WHILE MEDITATION WAS VERY helpful for supporting my well-being and personal transformation as I healed from the trauma, one additional thing I started hearing about from many sources turned out to be incredibly powerful - practicing gratitude. As an intuitive person who is also a scientist, I hear about things that are said to work, I sense in myself if they feel they might work, then I run experiments on myself to validate if they do work for me. Practicing gratitude was one of those things.

While being grateful is not a new idea, the deliberate focus on a gratitude practice was a new idea for me. I decided to start a gratitude practice six months into my healing process. I called it "30 days of gratitude" and committed to writing ten things I was grateful for about my day on my iPad every night before I went to sleep. With the understanding that nothing was too small to be thankful for (i.e., that it was okay to be grateful even for a good cup of coffee), thinking of ten things was pretty easy.

A typical list would look like:

> Nice run in the forest in the sunlight
> A good cup of hot coffee
> Big hugs from my kids
> Nice compliment from my colleague on my dress
> Great talk with my parents
> Finished my emails
> Fire in the evening in the fireplace
> Exchanged texts with my good friend
> Agreed to have dinner with an old colleague next week
> My children and I are healthy and safe

I felt good as I deliberately relived the best moments of the day through this practice. And when I was feeling down other days, I could look back at my list, and seeing it would make me feel better. I liked the practice so much that I kept doing it for another thirty days. After a few months I decided to commit myself to doing it for 365 days, and in the end, I did it for more than a year.

My gratitude practice evolved after that to become part of my daily meditation. Later, I realized I could also use it spontaneously to shift my mood. If I was upset in any way, the minute I felt I was upset, I asked myself, "What am I grateful for?" Then I would think of a list of up to ten things and feel how happy I was about those things. My mood would immediately shift. It was a great, positive way to change my attitude at will in the moment.

I also learned that expressing gratitude is an excellent way to lift up others. I believe that we never know which day will be the last day of our lives, so it's better to tell people that we love and appreciate them whenever the moment arises. It takes effort, however, to always be fully aware of what I am feeling underneath and to say what I feel to the person in front of me. It also requires some level of willingness to be vulnerable; it is something I continue working on. I can feel, however, the effect it has on me when people express gratitude for me and what I do and on others when I express gratitude for them and what they do.

Mu taught me that endings are even more critical than beginnings. When I left my company after 31 years of employment with them, I decided I wanted to express gratitude for everything I had received there. Since the company only typically hires at entry level from college, many people are with the company for their entire careers. People in the company become like extended family for each other, living through the ups and downs of life and supporting each other through them. As a result, sending a goodbye letter is common when people leave. Taking what Mu said to heart, I decided to express my gratitude to everyone who had helped me and for what I had received from my experience at work.

Here is the message I wrote:

Upon making my decision to leave the company after 31 years, a good friend of mine suggested I take two minutes to think of what I am grateful for from my experience working here. A flood of things came to mind instantly for which I am so appreciative: the company hired me in the US at the end of my summer internship, so I knew I had a job before I graduated - already a gift. Then after two and a half years, they moved me to Europe upon my request when I was 24 years old, which fulfilled a calling deep inside of me to relocate there; I could not explain this calling at the time, aside from feeling a strong desire to travel, learn languages and broaden my perspective in my personal life, all of which later came true.

Moving to Europe led me to so many beautiful things in my life, the most important of which was meeting my husband at work, marrying him, and having two amazing children. It also offered me the opportunity to travel all over the world and, further, to see so many cultures from the inside of people's homes, witnessing real life intimately in every region. It gave me the opportunity to continually learn and grow in areas I am passionate about including leadership, organization and people development, innovation and science and technology.

It gave me the opportunity to work with incredibly talented colleagues at the top of their field and together with them develop products that countless people all over the world use in their daily lives. It supported my desire to make a difference in diversity and inclusion and create human-centric work cultures. It challenged me to think big and supported my belief that nothing is impossible within the boundary of the laws of physics. It allowed me to make decisions every day which were entirely in line with my values, something I in no way take for granted. And importantly, it allowed me the greatest pleasure, of working with so many people - you and many others - who are so intelligent, principled, creative, inspiring and caring.

I have felt at home, like I really belonged here, from the day I first walked in the door. Thank you for making this experience so amazing; I am grateful to the company and to you for all of this. I am glad our paths have crossed. The many interactions and conversations we have had have deeply enriched my life.

All the best,

Heidi

I still include gratitude in my daily meditation, use it spontaneously to lift my mood if I feel upset, and try to express gratitude for others and what they give regularly. Overall, I have come to experience gratitude as a compelling way to bring love and light to myself and others around me. Gratitude is really a wonderful tool for all of us to lift ourselves and others up. What are some things you are grateful for today?

CHAPTER 8

Learn to Listen to Your Intuition

"The intuitive mind is a sacred gift, and the rational mind is a faithful servant. We have created a society that honors the servant and has forgotten the gift." - Albert Einstein

"Have the courage to follow your heart and intuition. They somehow already know what you truly want to become. Everything else is secondary." - Steve Jobs

I HAVE ALWAYS HAD a powerful intuition, even from childhood. I could ask questions and get an answer in my thoughts, immediately. I never thought much about where it was coming from, but over time, I learned to follow my inner voice and feelings as a matter of course.

My intuition is getting stronger, or perhaps I am tuning into it more, and I am using it as a tool along with my rational, research-oriented approach to inform my decisions. I am capable sometimes of asking for help or information relevant to making decisions in the best interest of everyone involved and getting 'downloads' of information as thoughts in my head. This experience and other feelings and sensations I have had while meditating have helped me to feel I am not alone, that there is a greater power - God, the Universe, our higher selves - that knows more than we do consciously, is benevolent, and is ready and willing to help.

I also learned that our bodies store information that our conscious mind cannot take in. I learned to tune into what my body was telling me. I started noticing I get goosebumps sometimes when I am talking to someone and telling them what I think is true or needs to happen. I sensed the goosebumps were a sign from my body that my instincts were right. I also learned to ask myself a question and could feel sensation in my body in one area such as my heart if it was right or in my stomach if it was wrong.

I heard someone at a conference once talk about getting a full-body 'YES!' when they feel strongly that they should do something. I imagined the feeling I get sometimes when I am passionate about doing something, like when I was a kid and was so excited about doing something that I was jumping up and down. I love this as a personal test when I am making decisions - I check in to see if I am getting a full-body 'YES!' inside.

I do believe in the mind-body connection and learned through Louise Hay's book, *You Can Heal Your Life*, what different pains or ailments in the body mean. Then if I was having any pain, I could mentally step back and say to myself, *Okay, that's what that means, so what needs to happen to remove that issue inside my head?* For example, I was having pain in my right knee as I was approaching a specific life transition. The right side of your body is associated with the action part of you and moving forward into the future. I then recognized that I had some anxiety about moving forward into the next phase of my life, asked myself what I needed to relax about it, and worked to put it in place. Once I did that, the pain in my knee disappeared.

I can look back on my life and recall times I saw images in my head or had feelings about what would happen in the future. Based on what has happened since, now I know they were real. Again, this helps the scientist in me looking to see if I can create validation. It's an ongoing experiment but one that already seems to confirm that intuition exists and has the potential to be accurate and helpful.

We can get better at tuning into our intuition through practice and through meditation. It is worth working to strengthen it and then running our own experiments to see when our intuition is accurate to build our confidence in it. Tuning into our intuition and then coupling it with our rational thought and what we sense our body is telling us can provide powerful insight. When we do this, we are really listening to our heart, mind and the rest of our body all communicating to us at once, giving us rich information about what is right for us. Take a moment to sense into yourself. What do you notice arising in your head, then in your heart and finally in your body?

CHAPTER 9

See and Trust Signs and Synchronicities

"As we blossom or awaken, we begin to notice there is a force in the world that seems to be operating and leading us into a certain destiny. And it's very much a kind of detective effort on our own part to figure out what these things mean. The synchronicity is essentially a meaningful coincidence that brings us information at just the right time." - James Redfield

"Synchronicity is ever present for those who have eyes to see it." - Carl Jung

ONE OF THE MOST unusual things that happened to me as I was healing and growing was that I saw the number 24 every-where. At first, I thought it was a coincidence, but then I started thinking about the role the number 24 had played in my life. I was 24 when I moved to Europe. My husband was born on the

24th; we married on the 24th; his phone extension at work was 2424; we were together 24 years. The number of times the number 24 started appearing on clocks, on street signs, on the computer, so many places all the time, made me start thinking perhaps someone or something else was communicating with me.

The phenomenon was so weird that I started taking pictures of it every time it showed up. Wanting things to work out with my husband, I started thinking it was a sign for me to hang in there, that he would change his mind and come back. After a while, however, I started thinking while it might well be something or someone communicating with me, that may not be the message being communicated - the message may rather be one of support, to keep going, that I am on the right path.

One of the funniest occasions the number 24 showed up was when I was taking my son to visit colleges in Colorado. We were on a road trip. He was napping in the passenger seat, and I was sending up a question to the Universe: *What should I do now with my life?* Then I came to a T-junction in the highway. My options were to turn right or left. The only signs directly in front of me were road markers: 24 East and 24 West.

I named the music publishing company I later started *Twenty-four*, and I ended up writing a song about it called "24." The lyrics follow:

<u>**24**</u>

If ever we had a number
It would be 24
Your birthday, our anniversary
Your phone number and more

Chorus
I keep thinking that we're over
That I should walk away
But somehow the Universe says
Stay woman, you must stay

The age I was when I came here
The years together now
The number of our lake cabin
24 take a bow

The number keeps coming at me
Relentless, day and night
The time, the date, even street signs
As if to keep me right

The time stamp I mailed my love song
Was 24 past 2
For me this number means one thing
The day the world got you

Bridge
Thinking should I take the life road
With you, or not, what's best?
My car comes to a T-junction
24 East and West!

So I am still hanging in there
Thinking, what is this sign?
That all roads will lead to you now?
No. That it's not ours but mine...

Once I realized signs can be all around me providing information, support, and encouragement, I saw more and more of them.

The most typical are the same number series (like 1111 or 2222) or the digits of my birthday. And 24 still shows up all the time. I never look for the signs; it doesn't work when I deliberately look for them. They just show up, and I always appreciate them.

People and opportunities also seemed to start coming into my life providing help and inspiration when I needed it and often in unexpected ways. Sometimes the synchronicities resulted in huge and lasting change. For example, Mu having an unprecedented window of time to work with me right when I reached out. Sometimes the synchronicities seemed smaller, but they turned out to provide just the support I needed at the time.

One such synchronicity happened when I was traveling to Portland, Oregon, to attend a long weekend class. I arrived at the airport at the tail end of a massive snowstorm in the area. I proceeded to the car rental place, thinking I would try to get an SUV, which would be safer to drive in the heavy snow. My class was an hour's drive south of Portland, and they hadn't cleared the highway there yet. I had made the kind of reservation where you can choose your car and drive it to the rental car check out. As I was walking up and down the aisles looking for an SUV, an attendant came out to ask if she could help. I told her what I was looking for, and she replied that she believed they were all rented out. Ever an optimist and very determined, I kept looking to be sure.

Then I heard a male voice with a thick Russian accent saying, "I can get you SUV." I could not see where the voice was coming from until a short, stout man emerged from behind a nearby car. It was not clear whether or not he worked for the car company. My stranger-danger-Spidey senses engaged; could I trust him? I then decided to lean forward and indicate interest because, if he was from the car company and if he could get me an SUV, that would be great. He said he would go out to the lot to pick it up for me, which I felt was very kind of him, particularly as the weather in the lot was pretty bleak.

At the same time, a tall forty-something man, built like a fit farm boy and dressed in a suit, was walking up and down the aisles. I heard him ask the attendant if she had any SUVs. She said she did not think so. As determined as I was to get one, he kept walking up and down the aisles searching for one. He and I were the only ones in the aisle. A bit of an introvert, I usually do not talk much to strangers when I travel. And I would never, ever get into a car with a strange man - deep imprinting from my teenage safety training, but something in me felt grateful to have that Russian man offer to get me an SUV. I had a feeling I was getting the last one. I also really only needed the car to get to my class, as a friend had already offered me a ride back to the airport at the end of it. So I walked up to him and asked him where he was going. He indicated a place that a quick search on my phone map app showed was an hour beyond where I needed to go on the same highway. I then told him I heard he was looking for an SUV; I had an SUV; and I would give him the SUV if he would drop me off at my class along the way. He readily agreed.

Getting into the car with a strange man driving me to my class was weird, but I have to say, we hit it off immediately. Within ten minutes of starting of the ride, we were trading life stories. He was from the Midwest too; his long marriage had also ended a few years earlier; he was dating a high school friend who lived in Colorado, and he was planning to move there. He gave me some good marriage separation related advice and safely got me to my class. I did not have to drive in what were some of the most challenging snow driving conditions I have ever seen. I did not need to rent a car. And I met a nice person who shared helpful advice in a great conversation.

This was an excellent lesson for me to be open to synchronicity and reach out in the face of it. My life since this incident has been an accelerating whirl of synchronous events which have brought amazing people and opportunities my way.

Signs and synchronicities all around us, all the time, and once we start tuning in, we see more and more of them. It is worth paying attention and then acting on them when it feels right as they can lead to powerful connections and learning experiences. What signs and synchronicities have you noticed appearing in your life?

CHAPTER 10

Love Yourself

"Wisdom tells me I am nothing, love tells me I am everything." - Nisargadatta

"Love yourself first, and everything else falls into line. You really have to love yourself to get anything done in this world." - Lucille Ball

FOR MANY PEOPLE, SELF-LOVE is one of the hardest concepts to grasp. I have had to do a lot of work on it myself these past few years. I was first introduced to the idea in a great book I read titled *You Are a Badass* by Jen Sincero. While I heard her say to love myself in that book loud and clear, I did not understand how much I needed it or how to do it. I filed that advice in the back of my brain as something that seemed important but which I should come back to when I could get more perspective on how to apply it.

Because thoughts and intentions have the power to help create our reality, I decided to at least start saying *I love myself* at the end of my meditation each day. And I figured out that when I am doing something stressful and demanding, such as finishing a hard run, what I am doing becomes easier if I say those words to myself.

Around this same time, I watched an excellent speech on YouTube by Marissa Peer, a top UK psychologist and hypnotherapist. In it, she tells stories about clients who have great fame and fortune but do not love themselves and are ultimately unhappy. She says that the number one human ailment is that we do not think we are enough. That rang true for me. One specific piece of excellent and practical advice she shares is to write on your bathroom mirror *I am enough*. I asked my kids if they were okay if I wrote those words on our bathroom mirror, and they agreed. For the next two years, the words "I am enough" were written in cursive in eye pencil on the lower side of our big bathroom mirror. I brushed my teeth and read it. I am enough. It was a powerful reminder for me as I continued healing and creating the next chapter of my life.

I also learned through my work with Mu and my therapist that my childhood wound is carried by my 'inner child.' Sharon, a psychologist, author, speaker and an external career coach I had five years ago, explained that when kids do not get what they need fundamentally from their parents, they blame themselves. I understood that it was a reptilian-brain-driven, survival-oriented choice children consistently make. For example, if a child is left alone to cry for extended periods of time, he or she could start thinking that the parent is not capable of caring for his or her basic needs. The child is extremely vulnerable and on some level senses that a parent not taking care of its basic needs could result in its death. This is such a threatening concept to the child that as a self-protective mechanism, he or she defaults to blaming himself or herself instead.

And as all parents are human and, therefore, imperfect by nature, kids are bound not to get all their needs met all the time. And so the child's self-blaming cycle takes hold. This helped explain to me what Marissa teaches about not being enough. In hindsight, I think neither my husband nor I loved ourselves enough to continue to be in the relationship successfully. It is somewhat of a tragedy when seen in that light, but it is also a lesson for which I am grateful.

Both Mu and my therapist taught me to imagine myself as a small child. In my mind, I am three years old. They encouraged me to imagine holding my toddler self and reassuring her that she is deeply loved and that she is enough. While it happens less and less, every time I feel now that I am not enough or not loved, I imagine holding my toddler self and reassuring her. It always helps.

There are small things we can do every day and on special occasions to love ourselves. They fall into the category of self-care and treating yourself. For example, make your bed every day. Making your bed is a powerful visual sign that you are caring for yourself. It also provides visual order in your home, energetically setting you up for better order and flow in your life. If you have a comforter with no top sheet, making the bed takes literally ten seconds.

Earlier I noted several positive, uplifting ways that we can take care of our body: eat well, exercise, spend time in nature, meditate/practice mindfulness. You can also treat yourself with small gifts, get a massage, take a long bath, eat dark chocolate, call a close friend, or listen to music. Read a good book or watch a great movie; comedies are especially good choices because laughter is great for your soul.

Make time to do more of the things that *you* love. Ultimately, an important aspect of choosing love includes choosing to love yourself, and you are the only one who can do that. What is one thing you can do today as an act of love for yourself?

CHAPTER 11

Forgive

"True forgiveness is when you can say, 'Thank you for that experience.'" - Oprah Winfrey

"Forgiveness is not always easy. At times, it feels more painful than the wound we suffered, to forgive the one that inflicted it. And yet, there is no peace without forgiveness." - Marianne Williamson

"To forgive is to set a prisoner free and discover the prisoner was you." - Lewis B. Smedes

WHEN I SHARED WITH a few of my friends that I had skipped over this chapter as I was writing this book because I was not ready to authentically write it yet, they offered some pretty funny suggestions, like I should write "F*@k it, next chapter." I do feel, however, that forgiveness is essential, and that it is critical to forgive others as well as yourself. I believe that the energy associated with the negative feelings linked to not forgiving others and/or yourself holds you back from being fully happy. That said, I confess this has all along been the hardest thing for me to do. So I will share authentically what my experience has been while fully admitting that I have not mastered this one yet. For me right now, forgiveness is a work in progress.

I think forgiveness is strongly associated with but not equal to my commitment to 'Choose Love' in the situation with my husband. Choosing love related first to my choice of action and second to my choice of thought - not always the first thought, but the one I consciously went to immediately after the first one. I associate forgiveness with a feeling, so it feels like the last bastion of closure in the situation. Because if I choose my action, then my thoughts, I expect the feeling, finally, will follow. I have tried to decide to forgive consciously. I have meditated often with the intention to forgive; in fact, over some periods I have meditated daily or even more often on this intention to forgive. But I cannot claim I am 100% there yet.

It feels easier, better now that some time has passed, but I still feel as if somehow I am waiting for things to be 'evened out.' The balance of giving and taking over time is a key principle for harmonious relationships. I recall telling the teacher who I learned this from that I felt like I could not get to forgiveness yet with my husband because the give and take still felt out of balance, mainly since he left out of the blue. She had an excellent answer that helped: she suggested that I also consider all that I have learned from the situation as a gift he gave me by leaving.

In my journey, I also started signing up for relationship advice from different sources online. I wanted to take responsibility for anything I needed to improve at by learning what I could about how to be great in relationship. I have actually learned a lot for which I am grateful. I recall reading somewhere that when your partner does something to hurt you, you need to see them as a small child, themselves hurt by people in their childhood eco-system, and to see that as the source of their action in relation to you. This is probably the frame that has helped me the most. When I think of my ex-husband as a small child, hurt in some way by others, I feel empathy for him, and it provides useful context for his behavior now.

We are all carrying around the context we grew up in and still practicing learned behaviors we used in our past to get our needs met. These past contexts also color how we interpret the actions of others. Seeing them through that lens, we often interpret the meaning differently than the actions were intended. Consequently, our reactions can lead to unnecessary pain and suffering for us and sometimes for others.

I believe that we choose others to be in relationship with who can teach us valuable lessons that we need to learn and to help us heal. Louise Hay and David Kessler said, "Every relationship is assigned to you for your healing." Sometimes I think that my husband leaving was an act of love for me on his soul level as everything that has happened since then has helped me heal in so many ways. I have grown in the last few years more than I have grown across the rest of my life. This experience has called me to reignite my spiritual side and grow in relationship with people I love in my life. It has led me to make some significant life changes that feel like what I am meant to be doing. I would not be writing this book if he had not left, nor would I have done so many of the things I am doing right now. I am truly grateful for what has happened since he left and the exciting future I expect lies ahead. This frame helps me to feel forgiveness as well.

The other frame that has helped me is the possibility that we have a blueprint for our lives, created before we enter it, that we have free will to follow or not once we get here and that it involves agreements that we have with others. I think it's possible that my husband and I had an agreement to have our kids but not to stay together for our entire lives and that we have other agreements we will fulfill with other partners as we move forward. This possible "greater plan" notion sometimes also gives me some peace of mind and makes it easier for me to feel forgiveness for him.

While forgiveness is often inherently very difficult, it is clearly part of choosing love and an important step in the healing journey for all of us. It is a journey in and of itself that often happens over time. And it is aided by looking at what happened from broader perspectives. Can you imagine a broader point of view for your situation which includes gifts for you and/or a potentially different and better future?

CHAPTER 12

Do What You Love

"Let yourself be drawn by the stronger pull of that which you truly love."- Rumi

"Doing what you love is the cornerstone of having abundance in your life." - Wayne Dyer

I DECIDED EARLY ON that one key to becoming happier as I was trying to cope with the pain was to focus on doing what I love. I have always loved to sing. It was not about performing, although I did a lot of that when I was young through musical theater, swing choirs, and occasional coffee houses. It was more about the act of singing. I loved to sit by myself alone in a room with my guitar, playing and feeling the music flow through my voice and my body. It was like I was transported somewhere else. I felt connected to something bigger, which felt amazing. In hindsight, I believe singing was a spiritual practice for me although I never conceptualized it as such in my mind.

When we first arrived in Germany, my husband invited over one of his school friends from Italy who had also relocated there. During her visit, she told me she was working with a singing teacher who was helping her with projection. This is one area I had always wanted to work on, so I asked for the phone number of the teacher. I put it on the bulletin board of our home office. I looked at that phone number several times a year, thinking I should call her and start taking singing lessons, then thinking my plate was overflowing and I did not have the time. I did this for eight years.

When my husband left, I decided I needed to do what I love. Finally, after so many years of having her number, I called the singing teacher, and she answered right away. I told her I wanted to take lessons and she invited me to my first one. She was kind, warm, full of light and talented, a Brazilian living in Germany. After a few months, she asked me why I was taking lessons: did I want to perform or do something in particular with my voice? I don't know where the idea came from, but the next thing I heard coming out of my mouth was "I would love to make an album." Now, I had NO expectation I would ever make an album. I did not think I was good enough and had no idea how to get it done. Nor did I have any idea what I would sing. I told her that studio singing sounded like fun, without the inherent stress of performing live in front of an audience. She listened and said, "Okay, I understand."

In the following months, I started writing music again - the first time since childhood - primarily songs about heartache and wanting my husband back. The song writing process was therapeutic, and creating something original felt great. I took my first song to my singing lesson along with my guitar. I asked my teacher if I could play her the song. She readily agreed.

After I finished, she asked me, "Where does that come from? Whose song is that?"

I said it was mine.

She asked me to play it again. Then she asked, "But who wrote the music?"

I shared that I wrote both the words and the music. She nodded and said she liked it.

The next week I came in with a second song. I played it for her. She looked at me, smacked her hand palm-side down on the table and said, "You have to make an album." She told me I had a sound that was both old and new and she could envision people listening to me on the radio, a mental test she used to decide about a student's potential. I told her I had no idea how to get an album produced. I asked her to help me, and she agreed.

Over dinner with my friend Emily in Geneva while on a business trip one evening, I asked her how many songs it takes to make an album. She said she thought it was ten. That gave me a target. I wrote 16 more songs in the next few months. My singing teacher then started telling me she wanted us to have a contract for what she would do and how any profits earned would be divided. Again, I had no expertise in this area, but was a bit apprehensive about entering into a contract and wanted to make sure I understood what I would be signing as it was a legal document. I shared the contract she proposed with two German lawyers. They both told me not to sign it as it was skewed too much in her favor; one of the lawyers said he thought the proposed contract wasn't even legal because of that.

When I told my singing teacher that the lawyers recommended I not sign the contract, she became agitated and then said she did not want to work with me on the album any longer. This was stressful for me, and by that point, I had enough stress in my life that it felt okay to walk away from doing the project with her. I was not sure what would happen next; however, so much synchronicity was happening in my life, I trusted that if I was supposed to make the album, somehow it would work out.

Soon afterward, I was telling Mu the story. She knew a studio in Boulder that she had had an excellent experience working with. She had hired them to do voice recordings of guided meditations for the class I asked her to teach my managers. I called up the owner of the studio, Geoff, who asked me to send him my work. I sent him fifteen MP3 recordings I had made with Garageband on my Apple computer, sitting on my bed in my bedroom. He wrote back, "Wow, very nice songs, and your voice is excellent!" and agreed to proceed.

I told him I needed a musician as well. He said he happened to have a gold record holding producer, David, who played a wide range of instruments who could produce and play on the album for me. I went in to meet them, and they were perfect. Geoff and David were terrific at what they did. I could not believe my luck. They were mentored by Les Paul, the musician and inventor who is in the Music Hall of Fame, and Larry Alexander who did sound for David Bowie, Eric Clapton and Bon Jovi. They were both so kind and grounded and took me under their wing like a little sister. They said they wanted to teach me how to make an album and have me be there for the whole process so I could participate in every decision. They were from the East Coast and Geoff's studio was built as a replica of an excellent studio where they had worked. I thought it was the coolest place ever and grew to love being there.

Over a couple of months, we made the album together. I was in heaven. I sang each song through twice and did the harmony parts David wrote for me relatively quickly. I loved that, but what I loved more was listening to David play the music for my songs. It was like continually taking a live music bath. And I loved watching Geoff and David work together. I could see they deeply respected each other and gently challenged each other to make sure the end result was great. David taught me that I could self- publish and copyright the music easily, and his wife helped me create my publishing company and get the album protected and published. It was a fantastic experience - a dream come true!

I sold some music to friends and family in my circle but still have to do what David said would be the harder part of the process: market it. I have put marketing on the back burner for now though as I feel called to do other things. For me this was a hobby and, while I am open to performing, I do not intend to make it my new career. But that said, who knows? I have decided you cannot predict your life. In college I never thought I would live in Europe for thirty years, married to an Italian. Five years ago, I in no way envisioned my life to be what it is now, so utterly different from what it was for the last thirty years.

Doing what you love is also a powerful aspect of choosing love. Deciding to do what I love led me down a path to achieving a dream that was bigger than anything I had even imagined. What do you love doing that you could do more of?

CHAPTER 13

Develop Yourself

"Knowing others is intelligence. Knowing yourself is true wisdom. Mastering others is strength. Mastering yourself is true power." - Lao Tzu

"There's only one corner of the universe you can be certain of improving, and that's your own self." – Aldous Huxley

I AM BY NATURE a problem solver and a personal development junkie. When my husband left, I looked for help. On top of finding my therapist and Mu and building my network of friends and family, I looked online. I do not recall exactly how it happened, but I found Mindvalley in early 2016. I love Mindvalley. It is an online, adult personal development learning platform, founded by Vishen Lakhiani, which "teaches you all the things you need to know that you did not learn in school." Their vision is to reinvent education. I signed up for course after course delivered by world-class teachers in areas I wanted to learn more about. I took Vishen's course which he later turned into his best-selling book,

The Code of the Extraordinary Mind. This course opened my mind to many powerful concepts about personal transformation.

I also took Marissa Peer's class where I was introduced to what she calls the most significant human ailment – to think we are not enough – and that it is critical to work on healing that. I took two of spiritual teacher Jeffrey Allen's courses on Energy Healing, where I learned more about what we are all capable of in terms of connecting with energy, healing ourselves, and accessing the information available inside and around us. I took Christie Marie Sheldon's class which focused on letting go of limiting beliefs within us that are holding us back from living extraordinary lives. And I took Deborah King's class, focused on spiritual transformation, which I mentioned in the chapter on meditation.

I also really enjoyed watching Vishen and his team grow Mindvalley. He and his team are exemplary entrepreneurs and fearless masters of fast-cycle learning and pivoting; they are continually listening to their customers and adapting to improve the experience for them. When I first started taking classes in 2016, a few hundred students were in the classes. A year later, thousands had enrolled. I recently saw that 180,000 have seen their latest masterclass and that they now have millions of students. Vishen and the team were able to grow the offering and the associated service quickly. They then created the concept of Mindvalley University, set in a different city each year for a month. The idea was to create what I would call a "pop up" University where people and their families could live and study for a month with a self-created curriculum crafted from the offerings.

I decided to attend in the summer of 2018 for two and a half weeks. It was an amazing experience. A community of 1000 people formed instantly. The community felt safe, filled with open people uplifting one another. It was multi-generational, multi-cultural and felt rooted in the desire to build a welcoming container of like-minded, growth-oriented, curious, loving individuals.

I attended classes of all kinds during my time there, from a four-day intensive with Jon and Missy Butcher to create a book for my life, my "Lifebook," with big goals and aspirations and plans to achieve them, to a two-day course taught by Vishen and his wife Christina to deepen my intuition. Witnessing how a community that feels safe, open, and loving can operate was inspirational. Many wanted to share their knowledge and gifts and were encouraged to do so by the Mindvalley team, on the condition they did not charge attendees. A rich, additional offering arose in real time, organically, around the Mindvalley University daily agenda. Talented, knowledgeable students offered free courses before and after the Mindvalley U day and on the weekends. It was a fantastic example of what could be - the potential to collectively create this kind of community in the world. They showed what is possible, and I am grateful I had the chance to be a part of it.

In addition to my Mindvalley experience, about six months after my husband left, Lisa told me about a nine-month-long class she was planning to take to become a certified practitioner in Family Constellation Therapy. It is a practice that helps make visible and facilitate opportunities to heal situations in family and relationship systems, often also including ancestral impacts. She had told me a little about the practice as she had learned it many years before from the person who created it, Bert Hellinger, as part of her graduate studies in Leadership and Organizational Development. I thought it was fascinating and was very interested in learning more. The class involved three face to face, long weekend sessions in Oregon over a nine-month period. I told her that I did not think I could take on that commitment considering everything that had happened in the past six months. She said she understood and let it go.

Several months later, before the class began, Lisa asked me again, telling me she thought it would be good for me. I declined again, saying I thought it was still too much to take on at the time on top of everything else. Then, a few days later, Mu called me to tell me that she was considering taking a class in Oregon, which her friend suggested that she might like. Mu told me she thought it would be good for me and that I should consider taking it too. It was the same class Lisa was asking me to take. Mu and Lisa did not know each other and did not know they were both encouraging me to take the same class. The class was small, sixteen students, making this coincidence even more remarkable. I felt like it was too much of a coincidence to decline the class and, with the support of my kids, decided to do it.

The class was perfect for me. The teacher, Jane, was academic and probably one of the best teachers in the world of the material. The class was small, which fostered an intimate learning environment. The other students were therapists and organizational leaders. The group felt very good to be a part of, another safe, loving, supportive container. The work was amazing, profoundly healing and transformative by nature. I took the class primarily using the practice to focus on my own healing. A year later I retook it, as did Lisa and Mu. This time I focused on more deeply learning the practice so that I would be capable of effectively leading others through it for their healing.

After the course, Lisa and I were able to lead a workshop with Jane at the European conference for practitioners in Germany. Connecting to the broader community of practice was lovely, and it was great to do it in the country both where the practice was born and where I had lived for many years.

I expect this practice will be an essential tool in my professional toolbox. I currently use it whenever I feel it will be helpful with friends who have important, deeply personal work to do.

While I feel that we all learn best through our lived experiences, and I was having plenty of those too, I was especially pleased that I had the chance to experience such rich learning online. There is great content out there, and a lot of it is free; it can be done in virtual community including interaction with other students, and it can be done any time of day or night. Heartache and life's invitation to transform offer profound opportunities for self-development, and there is a huge amount of high-quality content available to help us along the journey. We are lucky to live in a time when access to such content is so readily available. What are you curious to learn more about which can support your own development?

CHAPTER 14

Say Yes

"Say yes, whatever it is, with your whole heart and as simple as that sounds that's all the excuse life needs to grab you by the hands and start to dance." - Brian Andreas

"Respond to every call that excites your spirit." - Rumi

"Say yes, and you'll figure it out afterward." - Tina Fey

WHEN I DECIDED TO 'do what I love,' the other mantra I embraced to help myself was to 'say yes' to opportunities that arose that I would previously have hesitated to say yes to.

A small example of this was when my daughter's close friend's mom, whom I did not know well, asked me to go with her to a Kiss concert. I did not know if it would be fun, but she seemed like a nice person and I had decided I would say yes to opportunities, so I said yes. It was so much fun! We comfortably and spontaneously shared life stories at dinner and had a great time together at the concert. They moved away from Germany the month after we went to the concert, and we both wished we had connected earlier.

Another example came when I told a man I had sung with years ago in Brussels, Nigel, that I had released the album. I had connected remotely with Nigel only a few times in the twenty-five years since we had sung together. One of his hobbies was running a charity for children's cancer. As a singer and musician, he offered an annual concert to raise money for the charity. He invited me to come to Brussels to sing at his show.

While I might have previously hesitated to go (it would be a weekend away, and I would have to prepare for it) following my 'say yes' mantra, I instantly decided to do it. I asked Monika to come with me, and we had a wonderful weekend. Not only was the concert a huge success, with 300 attendees and beautiful music by many singers and musicians, but I also loved revisiting Brussels. And in beautiful synchronicity, I reconnected with an old colleague on Facebook the week before we went, and he offered for us to stay with him and his family that weekend. We had a great time. It felt significant to reconnect with him and get to know him as we are now, both evolved versions of who we were when we had worked together years ago.

There are bigger things I said yes to that I usually would not have: making the album and going to Mindvalley University in Estonia were two of them for which I am so grateful. Another big one occurred in the summer of 2017. My friend Lois, whom I had met at the Family Constellation course in Oregon, offered the idea. She lives in Boulder. I was visiting and had already decided I was falling in love with the place. While out hiking with her I told her I had a strong sense I might live there one day, that maybe Boulder was 'my place.' She suggested I find a way to spend a more extended amount of time there at once, 3-4 weeks for example, to try it out without yet moving there.

As I am one who thinks everything is possible, I started thinking about how that might work. I also wanted to take my son, who had just graduated from high school, to Machu Picchu that summer. I wanted to take a memorable trip with him to celebrate that milestone, and I had always been keen to go. I also wanted to be able to take the annual family vacation to Minnesota. I asked my boss if it was okay to take the two vacations and work remotely in between them. She generously agreed, which enabled me to spend three weeks in Boulder in between the two vacations.

That time was very powerful for me. First, the trip with my son was terrific; we hiked the Inca Trail for six days in what felt like a profoundly transformative sacred place. During the next three weeks in Boulder, I became more familiar with the city, and when I was not working, I recorded the album. Going to Northern Minnesota for the annual vacation to reflect, rejuvenate and reconnect with my family rounded out my time away. I returned to Europe with a deep understanding that I needed to be in Boulder. It really did feel like my place, and the people with whom I was connecting there felt like extended family.

Saying 'Yes' to these emerging opportunities was another way of loving myself and led to important further evolution of my life. We can all benefit from saying 'Yes' more to things that feel right for us. What is coming up in your life now that feels like it merits a 'Yes' from you?

CHAPTER 15

Be Clear About What You Want

"Often, if there's something that I want to do but somehow cannot get myself to do, it's because I don't have clarity." - Gretchen Rubin

"Clarity is the most important thing. I can compare clarity to pruning in gardening. You know, you need to be clear. If you are not clear, nothing is going to happen." - Diane von Furstenberg

I BELIEVE THAT BECAUSE relationships are made of a two-person system, I was partly responsible for what happened between my husband and me. After my husband left, I decided I wanted to work on myself before I dated anyone. I didn't want to be accountable for another relationship ending the way my marriage did. After a little more than a year of no dating, I decided I needed to start that journey. I had been entirely faithful to my husband in the time we were together, so I had not been with anyone since I started dating him, 24 years earlier.

The thought of dating was daunting, to say the least. I did not want to go to parties and bars to meet people as I am somewhat introverted and that isn't really my scene. I was also living in Germany and decided I did not want to stay there mid-term, so I did not want to date anyone there. I knew online dating was becoming more popular, but it also seemed scary. However, I had found our nanny, Maria, online on a nanny site and we love her; she is like a close family member. And she was the first person I found while searching on the site after sending out a request to the Universe to please send someone great. I invited her for an interview; she came the next day; and I hired her on the spot. So, online per se had been a good experience years earlier when looking for a nanny, which made me receptive to exploring online dating.

One evening when I was in Cincinnati for business, I opened my laptop and went to the only mainstream site I knew of. I studied the site from a product design perspective and concluded they had done a good job. All the key things one would want to know about a potential mate were covered - marital status (single, separated, divorced), kids, smoking, drinking, fitness, religious beliefs, hobbies, interests, and what they are looking for. I filled out the fields on the screen quickly; I was probably in there 10 minutes. I imported my Facebook picture. I used my own first name, not a big deal but I later learned, rare, and clearly a sign I was a rookie. Then I needed to fill in the city. I sat on the hotel bed, looking at the screen, unsure what to write. It was a US site, I did not live in the US, and 'national search' was not an option! I thought to myself, *Where do I want to live?* Boulder was the city I had fallen in love with, so I filled in Boulder. Then I closed the laptop.

The next day when I opened my laptop, I discovered a triple-digit number of men had responded positively to my profile. The sheer number of men showing interest in me was utterly overwhelming and very scary. It felt like Pandora's Box. I shut the computer immediately, not ready to deal with what I had created.

That week I had started making a list of what I wanted in a partner. There were 24 items including 'has done work on himself'; it was a tall order. Sarah had provided input, helping me make sure I had not forgotten anything important. By this time, I had started believing that the Universe listens, is benevolent, wants to help, and gives what you ask for if you have the right intention - so you need to be very careful what you ask for!

That weekend I traveled to Boulder. Lisa and I went hiking on my favorite trail in the Flatirons. I took the list on the hike and at the top of the trail, where there is a spectacular view, I called Sarah. With her on the phone and Lisa beside me, I burned the list, sending it out into the wind asking the Universe to please help me find the right person for me.

That evening, Lisa came over to Mu's where I was staying, and the three of us sat in front of the computer looking at the people on the dating site. I narrowed down my options to a few interesting people, one of whom I was strongly attracted to. He sent me a message a few days later mentioning that when I imported my picture from Facebook, it also brought with it the (8-year-old) subtext which said I was living in Germany and still with my husband. Another rookie mistake. I shared that this was old news. He asked if I had other photos of myself and suggested I post them on the site. I felt like he was trying to help me with the online dating thing when I clearly needed help, and that made me even more interested in him.

We exchanged a few more emails and then agreed to talk on the phone. The day we decided to talk I had had an argument with my husband that made it very clear to me that we would not be getting back together. The timing for that interaction could not have been better. When I got on the phone for the first time with this guy, I was open to seeing what might emerge. I immediately felt like we had known each other for a long time, and I could be completely honest.

We had a great conversation. He met nearly all the criteria I had on my list and a lot of others I could not ever have imagined. Not only was he handsome, but he was probably the most original person I had ever talked to - intelligent, kind, compassionate, funny, and extremely talented (he has won two Emmys for Directing). As for the 'working on himself' thing, he spent a total of nine years across a twenty-four-year period living in India studying with a teacher. And he's Canadian, so I could express my European side, baked in from 30 years of living there (such as randomly speaking French and using the metric system), and he totally got it. And as if all that wasn't enough, he lives in Boulder and loves it there.

Before we hung up, he asked me to visit him. I was able to fly through Boulder on my way back from a trip to Portland a month later. I would arrive at 10pm Sunday night and had to fly out at 5:30 the next afternoon. Because he had to go to work on Monday morning at 9, we had only a few hours. He suggested he pick me up at the airport and that I stay at his house in the guest room since we would have so little time to get to know each other. He was a stranger I met online, so that did not sound smart to me. We tried to figure out where else we could meet, a hotel lobby in Boulder possibly, but by the time I would arrive it would be close to midnight.

76

We continued talking and getting to know each other more over the following weeks. I started thinking perhaps it would be okay to have him pick me up at the airport as that would give us extra time to talk, but I was still not convinced I should stay with him. As the meeting neared, I told Mu about him and his invitation to visit. She offered straightforward and useful perspective: if he had spent nine years studying in India, he was unlikely to be a serial killer. I decided to go and to stay with him.

Meeting him in person was better than I imagined. He picked me up at the baggage carousel in the airport and, despite saying beforehand that he would not do it in the middle of the airport, he kissed me right there. There was clearly intense chemistry between us, but we were also both nervous and trying hard to make a good impression during that first meeting.

What would happen next wasn't clear when I left the following day. I wished that we had had more time together. I texted him this as I sat in the Denver airport waiting for my return flight to Germany. Unbelievably, one hour later, my flight was canceled and rescheduled for the next day. I called him, and he suggested I come back. That evening we sat on his couch and looked at the photos from his life on his computer. We had the chance to talk more about our lives, without the pressure of time and a first meeting. It was relaxed, and he felt familiar. It looked like there was real potential for a romantic relationship.

Over the next fifteen months I travelled to Boulder from Germany every chance I could to see him, Mu, and Lisa and feel what it would be like to live there. My relationship with him deepened. We enjoyed many romantic moments both exploring Boulder and staying home, talking for hours, cooking together, singing together, and one of my favorites, dancing in the living room.

While all of this was unfolding, I was experimenting with the possibility that we help create our reality through 'manifestation.' Can we manifest things in our lives? Having a new partner show up almost instantly through making a clear list, burning it, and asking the Universe for help was a positive check mark under the 'it's possible' side of the list for answering the question.

Another smaller practice I started doing, following an idea I got online, involved using an acronym as a password. The password can be used to name a goal, set an intention, or remind us of something we want to keep in front of us. I heard that it's also best to create the password in present tense as if it's already happening. Doing this felt strange at first, but I decided to proceed. I thought it couldn't hurt and maybe might help it happen faster, a 'pro' as I am impatient in general. I created an acronym around the wish to find love, be happy and grateful - tlihbhag: Trust love is here, be happy and grateful. I used that one for a very long time. It made me feel positive about finding love and reminded me to be happy and grateful every time I used it, which was many times every day.

A third example of something I did to get clear about what I wanted was deciding to take the excellent 4-day Lifebook course, created by Jon and Missy Butcher, with my friend Catherine at Mindvalley U. In it they have you think about twelve different areas of your life one at a time. They include categories such as love, parenthood, financial, social life, spirituality and career. You must decide what your ideal state is for each area, and you are encouraged to dream big. For each domain, you must outline why achieving these states is essential. You then describe your beliefs, ideally both those limiting and supporting achieving the states. Finally, you formulate steps you will take to realize these ideal states. The process was powerful. Since twelve areas are a lot to focus on, I chose five.

Four months later, I had completed my action steps for health and wellness and quality of life (home) with great results and made outstanding progress on love and career.

I do believe that being clear about what I wanted made a huge difference in enabling things to happen, but I also needed to take action myself for results to manifest.

It is so helpful for us to clarify what we want and why we want it. In which areas of your life would you like to be even clearer about what you want and why?

CHAPTER 16

Take Action - Fly Phoenix, Fly!

"Happiness is not something ready-made; it comes from your own actions." - Dalai Lama

"Throw your dreams into space like a kite, and you do not know what it will bring back, a new life, a new friend, a new love, a new country."- Anaïs Nin

I RECALL HEARING A story once about a person asking God why his prayers for divine intervention to win the lottery had not been answered. God promptly told the person, "You need to buy the ticket first." Being clear is critical, about what you want and, ideally, why having what you want is important. But it's your actions ultimately that make things happen in your life.

For example, I may never have met my new partner if I had not made the leap to go onto the dating site and register. I may never have gotten the help to heal had I not reached out to Mu or decided to use the support my company offered to get a therapist. I reached out to people to broaden my social circle and hosted a few social gatherings at my house, even though it was uncomfortable for me as an introvert. I decided to sign up for courses on Mindvalley and then go to Mindvalley University. Each time I used my intuition, felt into what my body told me and sensed what I felt in my heart, in addition to reasoning; I still do pros vs. cons lists to help make decisions. Ultimately, I followed my mantras of "do what you love" and "say yes."

After going back and forth for nearly two years between Germany and Boulder, it became clear to me that I wanted to live in Boulder. The next questions were: "How can I make that happen?" and "What is the right timing?"

Unbelievably, out of all the places my son could have gone to college, he decided that he wanted to go to college in Colorado. We had never been to Colorado together before he decided this. He had gone there for two summers in high school with his best friend and had fallen in love with the place. I took him to visit colleges there in the fall of 2016, a few months after I discovered Boulder and a year before I decided I wanted to live there. He went off to college in Fort Collins, Colorado, in August 2017. Now he, my romantic partner, Mu, and Lisa were all in Colorado. Still, I had a full-time job in Germany, and my daughter was there with me, going into her sophomore year of high school.

For the first time in my life, I hired a financial consultant to help me figure out if I could retire. I needed to know if I needed to find a job in Colorado or if I could afford to move and live there without employment. Several of my friends had already calculated at what age they could retire. I was not interested in and had never done that as I loved my work and wanted to keep doing it. But now I wanted to live somewhere else, where my company had no presence. To move to Boulder, I would have to leave the company that I'd worked for my entire adult life.

I had been saving money all my life, buying stock in my company with five percent of my salary every month for nearly thirty years. My European-sourced company pension, not yet available but ready when I turn sixty-seven, was secure. I had significantly increased my savings in recent years, and I had put aside enough money for college for the kids. I made a budget for my annual expected spending as requested by my consultant and, much to my surprise, he told me I could afford to retire. I was only fifty-two at the time, and I didn't want to stop working necessarily, but I loved the idea that I was financially free. That answered the question, "Can I move to Boulder?"

I told my boss I wanted to leave. I then talked to the head of human resources. I started crying on the phone, telling her I loved the company but wanted to move, so I needed to leave. She was great, saying, "Okay, just take a moment and breathe deeply." Then she and my boss and many others provided the amazing support I needed to leave the company gracefully. It was bittersweet. It felt like leaving an extended family. I had had good friends who had left and reassured me there was 'life after the company,' which helped. And I knew I would remain connected to the friends I had made at work over my thirty years there. So I set a date to leave in the summer of 2018, seven months after we agreed I could go.

I continued to travel back and forth between Boulder and Germany. Every time I landed in the Denver airport, I was ecstatic;

every time I touched down again in Germany, I felt like I did not belong there anymore.

The hardest part was related to my daughter. My ex-husband really wanted her to stay in Germany. She had been living with me for the past two years, seeing him one evening a week alone and once or twice a week when he would stop by the house. We asked a lawyer how we could decide where she would live, in Germany or in Colorado, and since we have joint custody, the lawyer said that we would need to ask a judge to decide for us if we could not agree. The judge would ask our daughter what she wanted to do and was likely to follow her wishes.

We immediately agreed we did not want to put her through that and decided to let her choose what she wanted. After many months, and some capitulation, she decided to remain in Germany and spend nearly all of her vacation with me. This was very hard for me. I seriously considered staying longer; however, I had not been happy for the previous two and a half years, and it would require an additional two years to complete high school - nearly five years in total in that state. One of my friends said, "You need to leave. Being this unhappy for this long can make you terminally ill." I asked my therapist what was best for my daughter. She said that the worst scenario would be to stay and be unhappy because my daughter could feel responsible in some way, feel like she needed to take care of me, and eventually resent me for making her feel that way.

While I hated the idea of being in a different country from my daughter part of the time, I felt that I really needed to move from Germany to Colorado and decided to proceed. I moved in August 2018. I think my son appreciates my being in Colorado, and I am grateful I see him often. While it is not easy for my daughter and me to be apart, we do talk and text frequently and, all considered, see each other pretty often as she has a lot of time off during the school year. Unfortunately, there is in this situation no perfect answer.

Since arriving in Boulder, my life has in other ways unfolded beautifully. My partner generously offered for me to stay with him. What felt like a temporary experiment has evolved into a lovely experience living together.

In the meantime, I also felt compelled to look for and buy a house. For a year I had been working with a very patient real estate agent, seeing hundreds of homes online and dozens live. One day I was driving down the street, having just seen another property, asking myself, *Why is it so hard to find what I want?* (I was very clear - I had a list!) The thought suddenly occurred to me, *You are trying too hard.* I decided I did not need a house urgently; I was delighted to stay with my partner and had no 'house emergency.' I decided to let go of searching and trust that the right house would show up on the right timing.

The next day a great house showed up on the market which, with renovation, would meet all the criteria. The seller offered to take bids for only three days. I put in a bid and won, with three other competing bids, even though mine was not the highest bid. I now own the house and have a builder-architect-designer team helping me create the renovation plan.

My partner was also scouting a co-working and social club space to shoot one of his shows in Boulder. He suggested I take a look at it for myself as a workspace. I went to see it and joined immediately. I now have a place to write and eventually work and am part of a fascinating professional community of like-minded, supportive people. I started helping a fascinating woman, an ex-journalist who has written eleven books and started eight companies, with a new business idea. She asked me to be on her board of directors. Getting on a board was something on my Lifebook action list that I had not started working on yet and, once again, synchronicity was at work!

Then I saw a flyer at the co-working space for a course called Theory U, taught by Otto Scharmer out of MIT which Mu had recommended to me. It was offered remotely, and a group was taking it together at the co-working space. I joined the group. My first ten minutes there, a man walked up to me to introduce himself as Elmar. I asked him what his last name was, and he told me: I recognized instantly that he was someone I had put on my mental list to meet in Boulder as he was an old friend of Lisa's and an expert at Family Constellation facilitation. We agreed to be study partners for Theory U and have started a delightful friendship. I had not actively looked for him in Boulder, but meeting him happened—more synchronicity!

I also started my own executive leadership consulting and coaching company, PhoenixRising. Supportive help showed up from many angles, right when I needed it, from legal and accounting advice to on-line platform creation to my first strategy consulting client, all within two months or so of deciding to pursue this new venture!

Soon after I arrived in Boulder, my partner took me to a colleague's garden party. To my delight, a small women's choir performed live music followed by acoustic guitar playing and singing. I met the choir director and a number of the choir members, who encouraged me to join. They seemed like a wonderful group of women. The choir teacher also teaches a great singing method to the group which is right in the area I wanted to develop further. I go every week and feel so lucky that I am a part of that warm, caring group. Lisa also invited me to join her in singing a jazz/funk/blues version of Handel's Messiah for the holidays, "Too Hot to Handel," with a two-hundred-person choir accompanied by the Colorado Symphony Orchestra. That has been a great experience as well. The level was close to professional, and the "sound bath" I experienced in the music produced by two hundred voices every week was amazing.

I was also interested in starting a yoga practice. I had tried one studio at Mu's invitation. The next time I wanted to go to yoga, I was driving towards the same studio and had an instinct to try another studio I had been to while visiting Mu two years earlier. I was keen to take up Kaiut yoga, which I had tried at the first studio. While the class name listed at the new studio for the time I wanted to go was not Kaiut, I still felt compelled to go. When I got there, I learned it was the same practice as Kaiut, taught by the studio owner, who infuses it with philosophy coming from *A Course in Miracles*. That sounded like a significant upgrade to me. The class was terrific, as was the teacher, and the fantastic mountain view out of the studio windows sealed the deal. As it turns out, four of the students there that day were in the women's choir I had joined! I now had a yoga studio to belong to.

I have also invested in my physical well-being and fitness. I took Eric Edmeade's thirteen-week long Wildfit class, which teaches about very healthy eating based on the way our hunter-gatherer ancestors ate. I loved learning about nutrition and food quality. I am now an avid consumer of high-quality, organic produce and very sensitive to sugar, which I discovered through eliminating it for six weeks is everywhere! I now try to avoid it as much as possible.

I also started 'slow' weight training with a trainer. This practice, also called Power of 10 or 10X, is the most efficient strength training program I have seen. It involves doing very slow repetitions for one and a half to two minutes on each of 5-7 different weight machines. This method is potent for building strength while being extremely time efficient. The recommended frequency is once a week, and it takes only twenty minutes.

Finally, I still run a few times a week and hike as much as possible. I am so grateful for the easy access to hiking in Boulder. Every time I enter the Flatirons, I am in heaven.

From love, to home, to family and friends, to community, career, and health and fitness, so many great things have fallen into place. I really do believe we cannot predict our lives. I never would have predicted all of this three years ago. If I would have tried to control things or make things come out as I had envisioned them back then, it would not have been this good. I am convinced now that we need to set an intention for good things to happen, practice following our intuition, focus on doing what we love, and say yes to what appears in our life that feels really right. We need to take steps ourselves in the direction we want to head, always be grateful for whatever happens and not be attached to any particular outcome because what appears could so easily be better than what we could ever imagine.

Much still lies ahead, and I look forward to what will come with time. I trust that what is meant to be will be and that, whatever happens, it will be good. I know now that even the difficult periods bring valuable lessons and other gifts to us. I choose love every chance I can, and I love as much as I am able.

I am so grateful for the people, the experiences, and the lessons that the most painful experience of my life has brought me. While I could not have known what would come three years ago that fateful day when my life changed significantly and permanently,

I can now feel joy and wonder, gratitude, and happiness in its wake.

I wish the same for you - for whatever challenges life has brought you. Know that you are not alone. So many of us are going through or have gone through heartache and difficult life transitions. Know that with these practices, starting with choosing love, for others and yourself, you too can get through heartache with grace, rise like a phoenix and fly into the next wonderful chapter of your life.

Are you ready to fly, Phoenix?

"A heart filled with love is like a phoenix that no cage can imprison."

- Rumi

Exercises

Chapter 1: Choose Love

While choosing love is often not easy, it is so powerfully healing and enabling. When you choose love, particularly in a difficult situation where you feel hurt or wronged by another, it fills *you* with love. It attracts love into *your* life.

Think of someone who hurt you. Make a conscious decision to be in that situation, in that relationship, with love. Decide to never say anything bad about them. Release the idea of retaliation. Release the idea you are a victim. Any time you feel like you are a victim, tell yourself you are powerful and you choose love. After a while the part of you who wants to retaliate, who wants to be a victim, gets tired and stops advocating for that. You start enjoying the benefits of choosing love. You know you are not a victim. You know you are powerful.

Describe below the situation for which you want to choose love. Write below it *"In this situation, I am powerful, I choose love"*. Sign your name.

Come back and read aloud this commitment to yourself any time you need to, to remind yourself to continue choosing love.

EXERCISES

Chapter 2: Get Emotional Support

We are not meant to deal with life alone. If you have people you know will support you, reach out and tell them that you need support. Ask as specifically as you can for what you need.

If you do not have people you feel you can ask for support, you need to start creating relationships that can offer you that. It is time to reach out. Start by making an offer, an invitation, by giving. Is there anyone you thought might be a potential friend, but you have not reached out? Ask them if they want to meet for coffee. Invite them to do something you both love to do. Or bring them something you think they might appreciate. Before I became friends with my neighbor, I heard she was not feeling well and brought her some soup. Just make an offer to open the door. Then as you get to know the person, tell your story. Be willing to be vulnerable. My experience is that when you open up, the other person often opens up too. And that can be the beginning of a meaningful friendship. It may not work with everyone you try with, and that's ok. Try with multiple people. As you keep trying you will start to build your support network.

Write here the names of three people you are going to reach out to. Describe what you will do or say to each person to open the door to creating a supportive friendship. In the next week, go do it.

EXERCISES

CHOOSE LOVE

Chapter 3: Get Professional Support

Sometimes we can really benefit from seeing professionals who are trained to help us. Ask family, friends or colleagues who they might recommend that can help you. Look on-line for local resources and read about what they specialize in, along with any reviews. Notice what attracts your attention and feels like a good fit. Contact them with any questions you have to help see what is the best fit. Decide who you want to work with. Make an appointment for your first session. If after a few sessions it does not feel like a fit, try someone else on your list.

Do the research above by asking others and/or looking on-line. List here below three options for professional help that feel right for you.

Complete your research by contacting them and asking any questions you have.

Circle the one you will start working with.

Make an appointment for your first session and go to it.

EXERCISES

Chapter 4: Mourn

We need to take time to mourn - to let ourselves feel our pain, to embrace it and to cry, which all help to release it.

Write below what it is you feel you need to mourn.

Take 10 minutes to think about it. Welcome the feelings that come up. Tell them that you see them. Tell yourself it's ok to feel them. Have compassion for yourself. Sit with the feelings for a few minutes. Let yourself cry. You are releasing the feelings, moving the energy. Anytime you start to feel the feelings come up again, repeat the exercise. After a while the waves of emotion around this which come and go should be fewer and farther between.

If you like, write how the experience was for you.

EXERCISES

CHOOSE LOVE

EXERCISES

Chapter 5: Take Care of Your Body

It is so important to take care of our bodies. Our physical health
and well-being can make or break how we experience life. Think
about the following categories that can directly contribute to
your physical health and well-being:

Sleep

Heathy diet

Exercise

Time spent in nature

Relaxation

Which category do you feel could use your attention most right
now? Circle it.

Make one commitment to yourself for a specific improvement
you will make in that area starting today. For example, if it is
sleep, a commitment could be to get at least seven hours each
night. If it is relaxation, it could be to get a massage every two
weeks.

Write your commitment here and get started with it.

EXERCISES

Chapter 6: Meditate

Meditation can contribute to well-being across many areas - ability to sleep, to remain calm under stress, to recover faster and better under stress, and many more. Choose one benefit you would like to get from meditation and write it here.

If you do not meditate, explore the different types of meditation on-line or through talking to others that meditate. Try one or more types, each day for a week, even if it is only for five minutes. If the first ones you try do not suit you, try another one or two the second week. Sometimes guided meditations can be very helpful to get started.

Know that it is totally ok if your mind wanders when you meditate. It's normal. When you notice it happening, just gently return to what you were focusing on in the meditation. Keep doing that every time it happens. Even very experienced meditators' minds wander sometimes.

List below who you will talk with to learn about different types of meditation. Contact them to start the conversation. After your conversations or, if you prefer, on-line research, list below three types of meditation that look interesting and try them.

Take notes for yourself about your experience and what works and does not work for you with each type of meditation you practice.

EXERCISES

CHOOSE LOVE

Chapter 7: Practice Gratitude

Gratitude is one of the most powerful practices to support healing and happiness. List here 10 things you are grateful for today. They can be small - such as a good cup of coffee, or a song you love that you heard - or bigger - such as gratitude for certain people or experiences in your life. As you write each thing down, take a moment to really feel how good it felt to you when you experienced it. Do this every day for a week when you wake up or go to sleep. If you are feeling down during the day, re-do the exercise and feel again how good the things made you feel.

CHOOSE LOVE

EXERCISES

Chapter 8: Learn to Listen to Your Intuition

Intuition is a powerful sense that we can all access and grow with practice. Think about a decision you are sitting in front of. It can be small or big. Write below the decision you need to make. Sit quietly thinking about it for a few minutes. Think about possible different choices you could make. Write them under the decision below.

With the first choice, take a few moments to sense in your body, how does it feel if you imagine you made that choice? Does it feel light or heavy, positively energized or tense? Where do you feel it in your body? Write what you felt as you did the exercise next to the choice. Think about another choice you could make. Sense into your body again. Record what you notice. How does that feel in comparison? A clear response either way for each choice provides additional information you can use to make your decision. Record below any insights this has given you for your decision.

EXERCISES

CHOOSE LOVE

Chapter 9: See and Trust Signs and Synchronicity

Signs and synchronicities are often happening all around us in our lives. Think about the last week, or if more helpful, the last month or the last year. Can you think of any fortunate coincidences you experienced? Where you were in the right place at the right time, experiencing something that turned out to provide you just what you needed? And/or do you see numbers like 1111, 2222, 3333, etc. or a specific number regularly when you are not looking for it?

Write below what you recall experiencing. As you go forward, start to take note when such signs and synchronicities occur. Be grateful for them, and they could well start occurring more and more!

EXERCISES

Chapter 10: Love Yourself

It is so important for us to love ourselves. When we love ourselves, we are more likely to be more successful, have more love in our lives, and be happier.

Make a list of three things you could do to love yourself more. This list can include, among others: better physical self-care (See Chapter 5: Taking Care of Your Body."); taking time for yourself; treating yourself; telling yourself you are enough regularly; telling yourself you love yourself; setting boundaries that protect you from others who may harm you; and quieting your inner critic.

Do one of these things for yourself today and start doing at least one thing to better love yourself every day.

EXERCISES

CHOOSE LOVE

Chapter 11: Forgive

Forgiveness is not easy sometimes, but it is very worthwhile to work on to support our own healing. Think of someone who you feel you need to forgive. Write their name and what you need to forgive them for doing below.

Hurt people hurt people. Think about this person as a small child being hurt by someone else. Allow yourself to feel compassion for that hurt child.

Then think about what good might happen out of the situation you need to forgive the person for. What lessons might be learned? What changes might be made that otherwise might not have happened?

Now think about how holding onto the negative feelings about the situation is affecting you.

Decide to forgive the person.

And if it still feels too early to fully forgive, come back to this exercise later.

CHOOSE LOVE

EXERCISES

Chapter 12: Do What You Love

One sure gateway to increased happiness and well-being is to regularly do what you love. Write down three things you love doing. If you cannot easily come up with them, think about what you loved doing as a child and write that down. Decide you will do at least one of these things in the next week. Circle that one and do it. Then commit to doing at least one thing you love every week, ideally more often.

EXERCISES

CHOOSE LOVE

Chapter 13: Develop Yourself

What are you curious to learn more about? Who have you heard about that you feel attracted to learning from? Look on-line or ask others you know for recommendations. Books, audiobooks, podcasts, YouTube videos, TedX speeches, online learning platforms like Mindvalley and live lectures and classes are all great places to learn.

List three things below you would like to learn more about. For each item, research where you can find material to learn about it. List what you will read, listen to, watch or attend live. Do so in the next two weeks for the topic you are most interested in.

CHOOSE LOVE

EXERCISES

Chapter 14: Say Yes

Next time you have an opportunity to do something (that could be good for you) that you normally would decline, say yes.

Write about what happens here.

EXERCISES

CHOOSE LOVE

Chapter 15: Get Clear About What You Want

Think about something you want to manifest in your life. It could be in any area - work, love, friendship, a creative achievement, financial gain, etc. Make a list of traits you want it to include. Be as complete as possible. Take a few minutes to imagine it is already true. Focus on how good you feel having that in your life.

Write the area you are focusing on and the list of traits you want it to include below. If you like, also write it on another piece of paper and safely burn it, releasing your desire to a higher power, requesting support for it to enter your life it and trusting it or something better will appear.

CHOOSE LOVE

EXERCISES

Chapter 16: Take Action - Fly Phoenix Fly!

You can be clear about what you want, but to get it you also need to take action. Think about what you asked for in the exercise above. Write below three things you can do to help your wish materialize. Can you ask someone for help? Can you make yourself more ready in any way for the opportunity? Can you find others who might be looking for someone like you as, for example, an employee, partner, friend, or creative talent? Take at least one action step this week to make your desire come true.

Acknowledgments

I WOULD LIKE TO thank my family and friends who supported me through my difficult life transition and helped me emerge like a phoenix into the next chapter of my life. They lovingly, metaphorically, and literally held me through the journey.

Thank you to my partner, who led me to love again and powerfully supports me in being the best version of myself.

Thank you to my ex-husband, who chose love along with me through our separation.

Thank you, Wilbur, my first, third and fifth boss, who taught me how to write.

Thank you to my coach, editor and a great end-to-end support for the book, Mary Lou Kayser; I could not have done it without you!

Resources

Omvana - www.omvana.com

Jen Sincero -www.jensincero.com

Mindvalley - www.mindvalley.com

Lifebook - www.mindvalley.com/lifebook/online

Marisa Peer - zwww.marisapeer.com

Wildfit with Eric Edmeades - www.getwildfit.com

Powerpath Monthly Forecasts - www.thepowerpath.com

How to Connect with Heidi and become part of the *Choose Love* Tribe

I would love to hear from you! Please let me know what you think of *Choose Love* and how your Choose Love journey is going.

Website - www.chooselovetribe.com, www.heidipiper.com, www.phoenixrisingco.com

Like and follow my Facebook author page - www.fb.me/chooselovephoenixrising

Sign up for my email posts - chooselovetribe.com/signup

Contact me by email - chooselove@phoenixrisingco.com

Follow me on Instagram - @ heidi.piper

Listen to my album *Lovers and Friends* - available on-line through CDbaby, Amazon, iTunes, Spotify and many other online sites which sell and stream music.

I would like to facilitate creation of a **Choose Love** Tribe where like-minded people come together to share stories and support each other on their journeys. Would you like to join?

Join the Choose Love Tribe on my author facebook page.

Let's start a Choose Love Movement! Here are some ideas:

Encourage others to Choose Love too. Share your own Choose Love stories on Facebook and Instagram using #chooselovestory and #Ichooselove

Share your stories related to the book with #chooselovebook and #Iamaphoenix, and with the practices associated with each chapter with the following hashtags:

#chooselove
#getemotionalsupport
#getprofessionalsupport
#mourn
#takecareofyourbody
#meditate
#practicegratitude
#learntolistentoyourintuition
#seeandtrustsignsandsynchronicity
#loveyourself
#forgive
#dowhatyoulove
#developyourself
#sayyes
#getclearaboutwhatyouwant
#takeactionflyphoenixfly!

Come to the edge.
We might fall.

Come to the edge.
It's too high!

Come to the edge.
And they came.

And he pushed.
And they flew.

- Guillaume Apollinaire

CPSIA information can be obtained
at www.ICGtesting.com
Printed in the USA
LVHW040432291019
635549LV00004B/1301/P